BASTIEN

PIANO FOR ADULTS
A Beginning Course: Lessons ◆ Theory ◆ Technic ◆ Sight Reading

Jane Smisor Bastien, Lisa Bastien, & Lori Bastien

Preface

We are thrilled that you have decided to add piano to your life! Whether this is your first attempt, or you are taking a refresher course, we hope you will find this experience fun and fulfilling. We wish you all the best in your endeavor.

Sincerely,
Jane Smisor Bastien, Lisa Bastien, and Lori Bastien

Table of Icons

 This icon is used as a reminder to check your answers in the answer key. The answer key may be found on page 152.

 This icon is used whenever any new notes are presented.

 This icon is used when a historical or theoretical piece of information is given.

 This icon is used to review important information which has been presented previously.

 This icon is used whenever follow-up exercises are presented.

 This icon is used as a reminder to locate the starting notes in each hand before playing.

 This icon is used to indicate pieces that have *Accompaniment Recordings* available through the IPS (see instructions on the inside front cover how to access). The recordings are also available separately in a 2-CD pack (KP1CD). The circled number inside the icon indicates the particular CD track on Disc One or Disk Two.

ISBN 0-8497-7300-8

CONTENTS

CHAPTER 6 - New Rhythms

CHAPTER 7 - Reading in F

CHAPTER 8 - Scales, Chords and Inversions

Chapter 1

An Introduction to the Piano

- ◆ Posture and Sitting Position
- ◆ Finger Numbers
- ◆ Hand Position
- ◆ Keyboard Geography
- ◆ The Music Alphabet
- ◆ Basic Rhythm
- ◆ C 5-Finger Position
- ◆ C Chord
- ◆ Repeat Sign

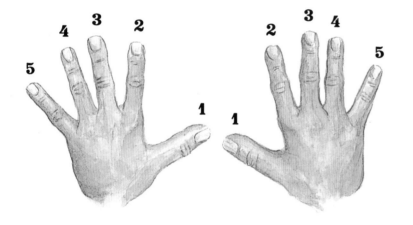

Posture and Sitting Position

- ◆ Sit a comfortable distance from the piano with your knees slightly under the keyboard.
- ◆ Sit up straight, relax your shoulders, and lean your upper torso slightly forward.
- ◆ Keep your elbows slightly higher than the keys and your wrists level with your forearms.

Finger Numbers

- ◆ Say these finger numbers aloud, moving the corresponding fingers.
- ◆ Learn these finger numbers so your response becomes automatic.

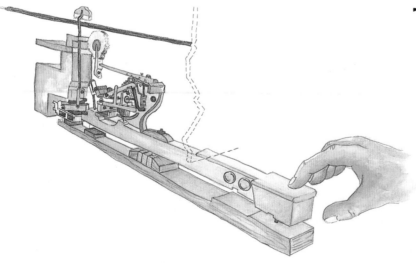

Tone

- ◆ When a key is pressed down, a hammer inside the piano strikes two or three strings to make a sound of a definite pitch.
- ◆ We call this sound **tone**.

Hand Position

A good hand position with curved fingers is extremely important when playing the piano.
Playing with curved fingers:
- Allows all fingers to function properly and efficiently together.
- Is essential in order to maintain control and consistency of sound.

Loose Fist Technic

To prepare for a hand position with good shape and form, begin by making
a loose fist with your Left Hand (L.H.).

Practice Suggestions

1. Place your L.H. fist on any group of 3 black keys.
2. Decide whether you want the tones to sound loud or soft.
   Play two different ways:
   a. To make a **louder sound**, sink **quickly** into the keys.
   b. To make a **softer sound**, sink **slowly** into the keys.
3. After the tones are heard, roll your hand forward and
   upward in a relaxed and gentle manner. The wrist should
   lead.
4. Repeat this exercise with your Right Hand (R.H.).

First Joint Technic

- The first joints of fingers 2, 3, 4, and 5 help control the beauty
  of tone and consistency of sound.
- The first joint technic uses the thumb to support the first joint of
  fingers 2, 3, 4 and 5 as shown in the diagram.

Practice Suggestions

1. Place your supported L.H. second finger on any black key.
2. Decide whether you want the tone to sound loud or soft. Play.
3. After the tone is heard, roll your hand forward and upward
   in a relaxed and gentle manner. The wrist should lead.
4. Repeat this exercise with your R.H. second finger.
5. Repeat this exercise with fingers 3, 4, and 5 in both hands.

Tennis Ball Image

- After you feel comfortable with the "Loose Fist" and "First
  Joint" technics, make a loose fist with your L.H. and place
  your hand and wrist on the table.
- Slowly open your hand and imagine that you are holding a
  tennis ball with a loose, relaxed grip.
- Picture this "tennis ball" image as you play the piano,
  continuing to keep your fingers gently curved.

Keyboard Geography

◆ A complete working knowledge of keyboard geography is essential when playing the piano.
◆ The acoustic piano keyboard has a pattern of 88 black and white keys.
◆ The black keys are grouped in sets of twos and threes.

◆ Tones sound **higher** as you move **up** (to the right) on the keyboard.
◆ Tones sound **lower** as you move **down** (to the left) on the keyboard.

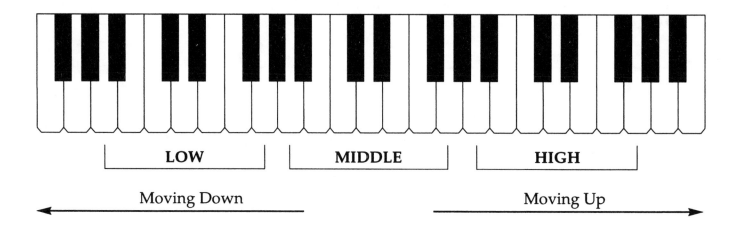

| LOW | MIDDLE | HIGH |

Moving Down ←   Moving Up →

---

2 Black-Key Groups Moving Up

1. **LEFT HAND: Play fingers 3 and 2 together.** Beginning in the low section of the keyboard, play all the groups of 2 black keys **moving up** until reaching the middle section of the keyboard.

2. **RIGHT HAND: Play fingers 2 and 3 together.** Beginning in the middle section of the keyboard, continue playing all the groups of 2 black keys **moving up** the keyboard.

---

3 Black-Key Groups Moving Down

1. **RIGHT HAND: Play fingers 2, 3, and 4 together.** Beginning in the high section of the keyboard, play all the groups of 3 black keys **moving down** until reaching the middle section of the keyboard.

2. **LEFT HAND: Play fingers 4, 3, and 2 together.** Beginning in the middle section of the keyboard, continue playing all the groups of 3 black keys **moving down** the keyboard.

The Music Alphabet

- The Music Alphabet names the white keys on the keyboard: **A B C D E F G**.
- The same seven keys, **A B C D E F G**, are repeated all the way up the keyboard.

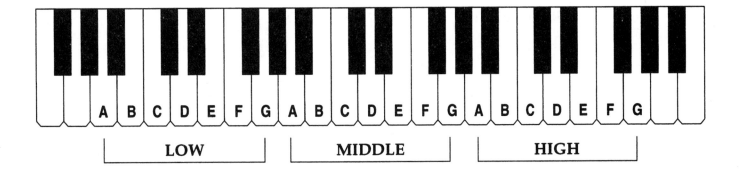

LOW   MIDDLE   HIGH

Practice Suggestions

1. Using the L.H. second finger, find an **A** in the low section on the keyboard. Play the seven keys in the music alphabet both up and down the keyboard, saying the letter names of the keys aloud as you play.
2. Using the R.H. second finger, repeat this exercise in the middle and high sections of the keyboard.
3. Begin with the lowest A:
   - Using the L.H. second finger, play all the A's in the low and middle sections on the keyboard.
   - Using the R.H. second finger, play all the A's in the middle and high sections on the keyboard.
4. Repeat this exercise with the other individual white keys: **B C D E F G**.

- Individual white keys are located by referring to groups of two and three black keys.
- Be able to verbalize where the white keys are in relationship to the surrounding black keys. For example, "D is between the 2 black-key group."
- Memorize the location of each white key.

A is between the top two black keys of each 3 black-key group.

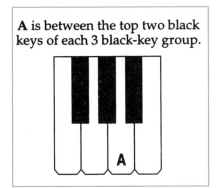

B is to the right of each 3 black-key group.

C is to the left of each 2 black-key group.

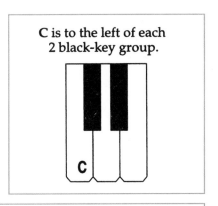

D is between each 2 black-key group.

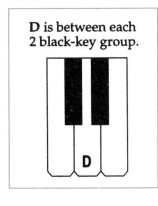

E is to the right of each 2 black-key group.

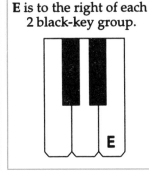

F is to the left of each 3 black-key group.

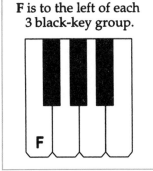

G is between the bottom two black keys of each 3 black-key group.

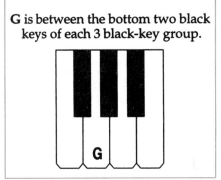

KP1

Basic Rhythm

Music is made up of short and long tones. Notes symbolize the duration of each tone. This combination of short and long tones is called **rhythm**.

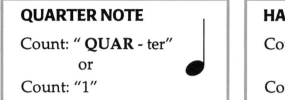
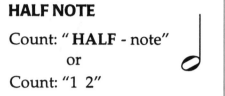

QUARTER NOTE

Count: " **QUAR** - ter"

or

Count: "1"

HALF NOTE

Count: " **HALF** - note"

or

Count: "1 2"

Practice Suggestions

1. Clap and count the following rhythms aloud. Keep a steady beat.
2. Practice playing the following rhythms with either hand in the middle section of the keyboard using the indicated keys and finger numbers.
3. Count aloud while playing and hold each note for its full value. Keep a steady beat.

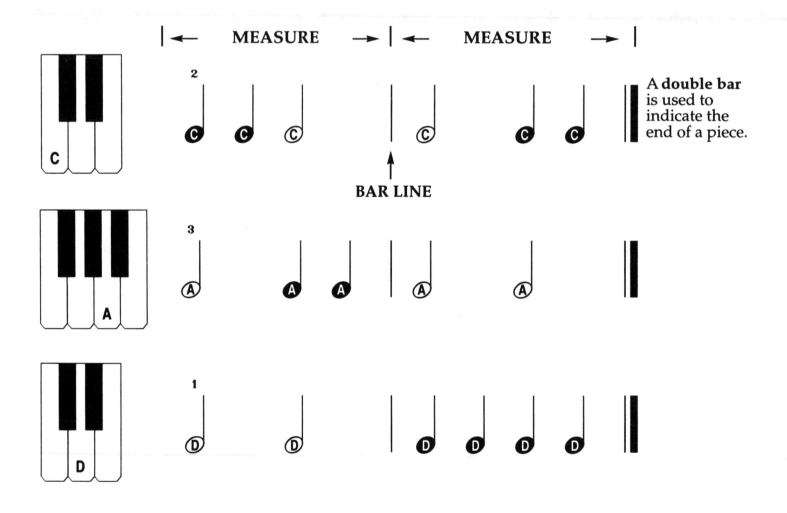

A **double bar** is used to indicate the end of a piece.

BAR LINE

Each measure contains the same number of beats.

Review

Write the letter names of each shaded key in the blanks provided.

1.  ___

2. 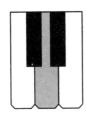 ___

3. 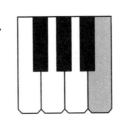 ___

4.  ___

5. 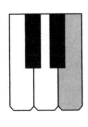 ___

6. 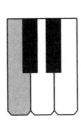 ___

7. 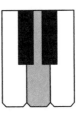 ___

8. 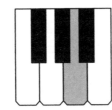 ___

9.  ___

10.  ___

11. 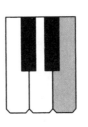 ___

12.  ___

13.  ___

14. 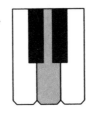 ___

15.  ___

16.  ___

KP1

Review

A. Without looking at the keyboard, fill in the letter names of the white keys in the blanks provided.

1. _____ is between each 2 black-key group.
2. _____ is to the right of each 3 black-key group.
3. _____ is between the bottom two black keys in each 3 black-key group.
4. _____ is to the left of each 2 black-key group.
5. _____ is between the top two black keys each 3 black-key group.
6. _____ is to the right of each 2 black-key group.
7. _____ is to the left of each 3 black-key group.

B. Identify the following notes:

1. _____   2. _____

C. Play in Rhythm:
1. Clap and count the following rhythms aloud. Keep a steady beat.
2. Practice playing the following rhythms with either hand in the middle section of the keyboard using the indicated keys and finger numbers.
3. Count aloud while playing and hold each note for its full value. Keep a steady beat.

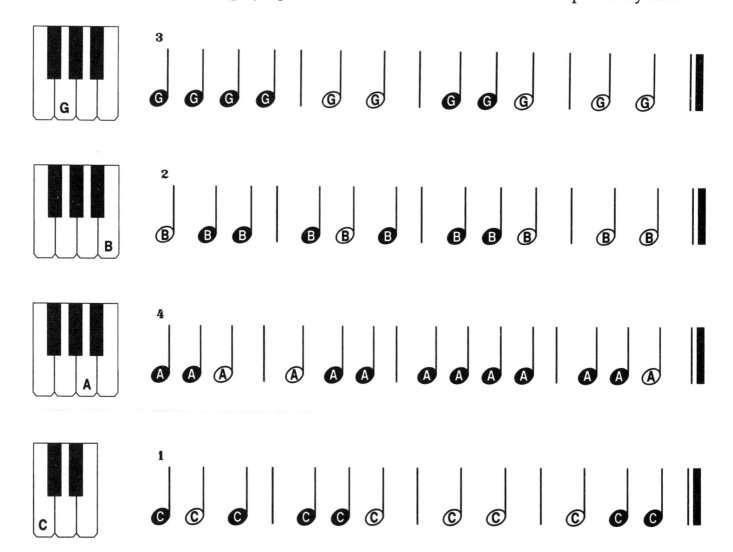

C 5-Finger Position

The first pieces you play will be in the C 5-Finger Position.
Each hand uses the same five keys: C, D, E, F, and G in two different places on the keyboard.

C 5-Finger Position

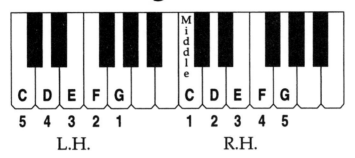

Use the following practice suggestions throughout Chapter 1.

Prepare to Play

1. Clap and count the rhythm aloud.
2. Find the C 5-Finger Position:
   R.H. 1 on Middle C.
   L.H. 5 on the C below Middle C.

Play 3 Different Ways

1. Play and say the finger numbers aloud.
2. Play and count the rhythm aloud.
3. Play and say the letter names aloud.

Always Remember

1. Keep a good hand position as you play.
2. Keep your eyes on the music.

ETUDE IN C

Etude is a French word meaning "study."

Position: C 5-Finger

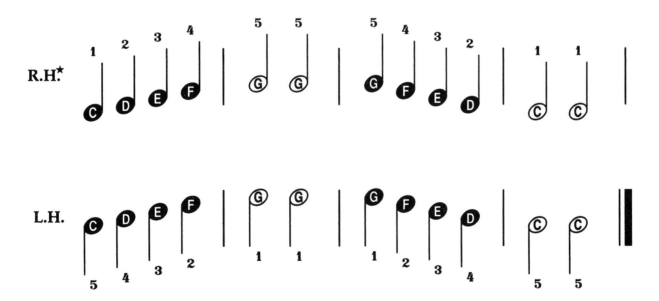

★ In **pre-staff notation:** the R.H. plays the notes with stems going up.
the L.H. plays the notes with stems going down.

Ludwig van Beethoven (1770 - 1827), German composer, studied piano with Haydn and began his career as a promising virtuoso pianist and composer. His increasing deafness at the age of 31 however, forced him to give up playing the piano in public and drove him to pursue composing with an unprecedented passion. A prolific composer, Beethoven wrote thirty-two piano sonatas, five piano concertos, one violin concerto, an opera, a great quantity of chamber music, symphonies, and many other works. An excerpt from his dramatic *Symphony No. 9* appears below. Beethoven conducted the premiere performance of *Symphony No. 9* on May 7, 1824, in Vienna. Milton Cross, author of *Milton Cross' Encyclopedia Of The Great Composers And Their Music*, wrote: "The symphony ended. But Beethoven, who had heard nothing – and who was several measures off – continued conducting even as the applause erupted. At last the contralto, Caroline Ungher, walked over to the master and gently turned him around to the demonstrative audience."

ODE TO JOY

Position: C 5-Finger

Ludwig van Beethoven

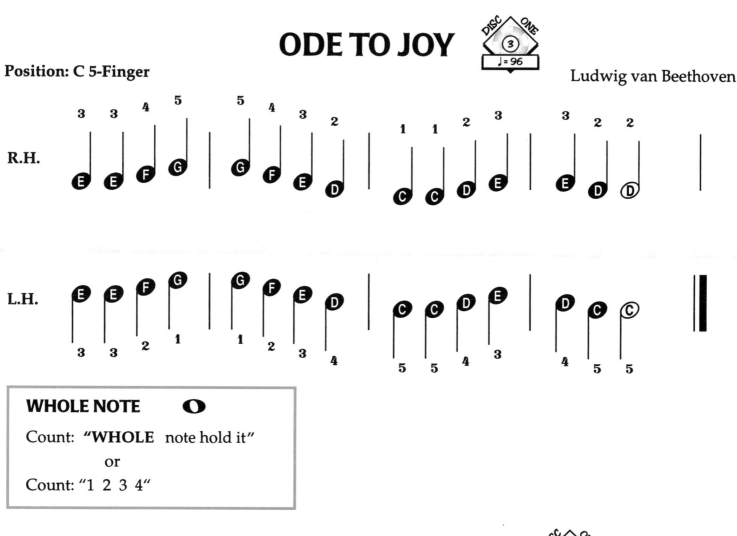

WHOLE NOTE 𝕺

Count: **"WHOLE** note hold it"

or

Count: "1 2 3 4"

AU CLAIR DE LA LUNE

Position: C 5-Finger

French Folk Song

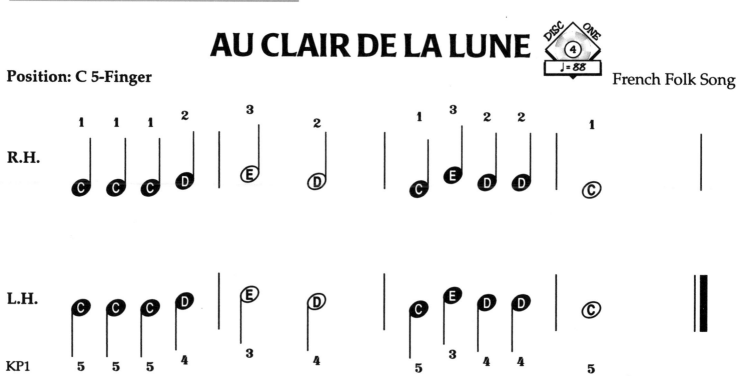

GOOD KING WENCESLAS

Position: C 5-Finger

Traditional Carol

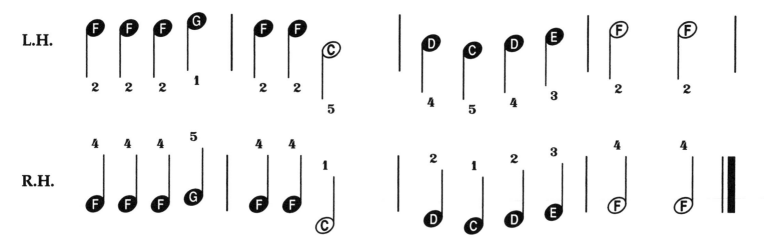

In **pre-staff notation:** the R.H. plays the notes with stems going up.
the L.H. plays the notes with stems going down.

Note: In *Frère Jacques* you will change hands within a measure for the first time.

FRÈRE JACQUES

Position: C 5-Finger

French Folk Song

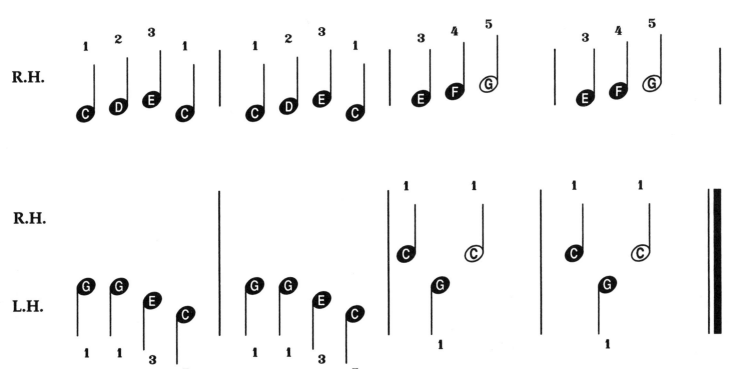

KP1

The C Chord

The **C Chord** is formed from three of the keys in the **C 5-Finger Position**: C E G.

Block Chord: Notes in a chord played simultaneously.

Broken Chord: Notes in a chord played one at a time.

DOTTED HALF NOTE

Count: **"Half** - note - dot"

or

Count: **"1 2 3"**

The repeat sign means to repeat (play again) from the beginning of the piece.

GENTLE WAVES

DISC ONE ♩ = 80

Position: C 5-Finger

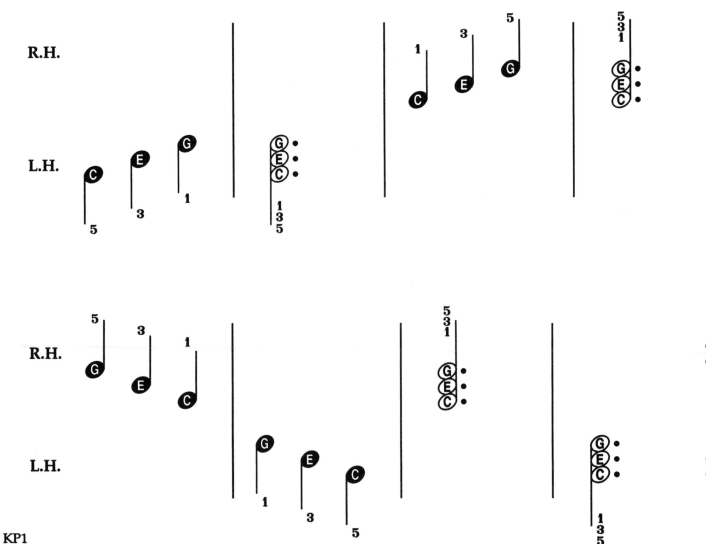

KP1

Review

A. Write the letter names of each shaded key in the blanks provided.

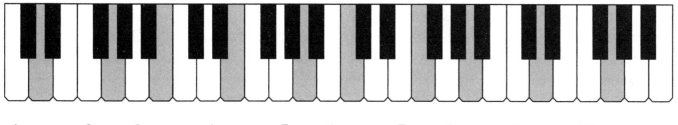

1. ___   2. ___ 3. ___   4. ___   5. ___ 6. ___   7. ___ 8. ___   9. ___   10. ___

B. On the keyboard to the right:
   1. Write the letter names on the keys to form the C 5-Finger Position with both hands.
   2. Shade the three keys to form C chords for both hands.

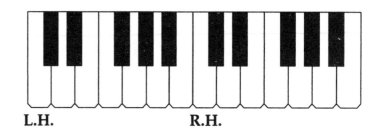

L.H.   **R.H.**

C. Draw the following notes:

   1. Quarter Note _____   2. Half Note _____   3. Dotted Half Note _____   4. Whole Note _____

D. Play the following C chords. Count aloud as you play.

BLOCK AND BROKEN CHORDS

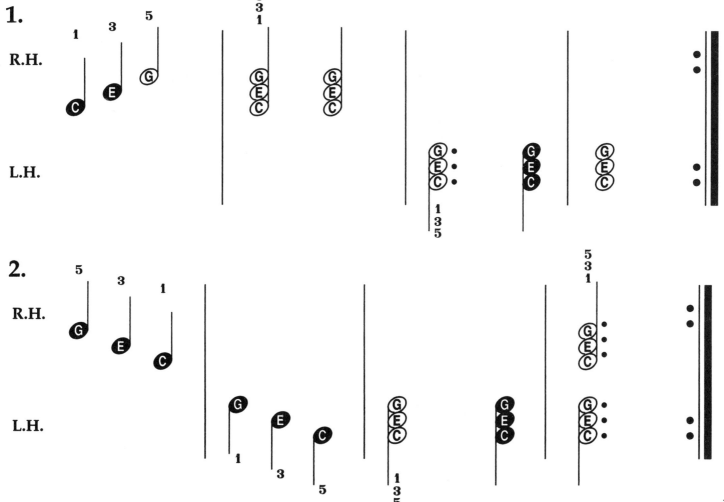

Chapter 2
Music Notation

- ◆ Notes on the Staff
- ◆ Time Signatures $\frac{3}{4}$ $\frac{4}{4}$
- ◆ Rests
- ◆ Melodic & Harmonic Intervals: 2nd, 3rd, 4th, and 5th
- ◆ Dynamics
- ◆ Damper Pedal
- ◆ Slurs and Ties

Treble and Bass Staffs

- ◆ Music is written on lines and spaces called a staff.
- ◆ Notes are written:
   1. On the **5 lines**.
   2. In the **4 spaces** between the lines.
   3. In the spaces above and below the staff.
   4. On ledger lines (short lines added above or below the staff).

space above

space below   ledger line

- ◆ Piano music uses two clefs:

   Treble Clef or **G Clef** sign: **Bass Clef** or **F Clef** sign:

- ◆ Middle and high tones are written on the **treble staff**.
   Notes written on the treble staff are usually played by the R.H.

- ◆ Low and middle tones are written on the **bass staff**.
   Notes written on the bass staff are usually played by the L.H.

C 5-Finger Position on the Grand Staff

- ◆ The treble staff and the bass staff are joined together by a **brace** to form the **Grand Staff**. Below are the notes in the **C 5-Finger Position**. Memorize the letter names and their placement on the **Grand Staff**.

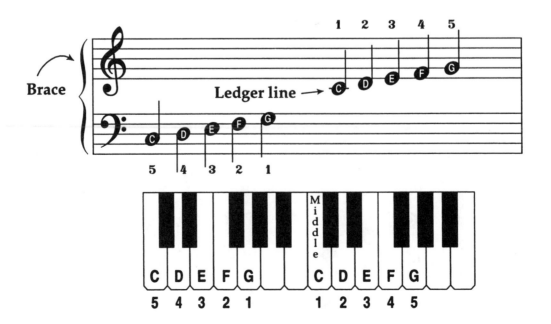

Time Signature

- The two numbers written at the beginning of each piece are called the time signature.
- The upper number indicates the number of beats (or counts) in each measure.
- The lower number indicates what kind of a note gets one beat (or count).

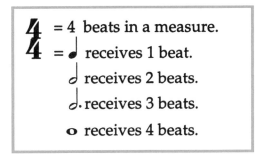

$\frac{4}{4}$ = 4 beats in a measure.

= ♩ receives 1 beat.

♩ receives 2 beats.

♩. receives 3 beats.

o receives 4 beats.

Follow these practice suggestions throughout the rest of the book:

Practice Suggestions

1. Write the counts in the music (1 2 3 4).
2. Clap and count the rhythm aloud.
3. Find your position on the keyboard.
4. Play and sing (or say) the letter names aloud.
5. Play and count the rhythm aloud.

 Stem rule: Any note on or above the middle line of the staff has a stem going down on the left side of the note head. Any note on or below the middle line of the staff has a stem going up on the right side of the note head.

PRELUDE IN C

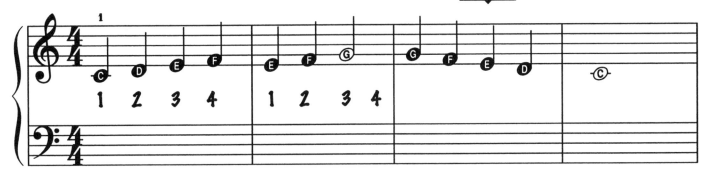

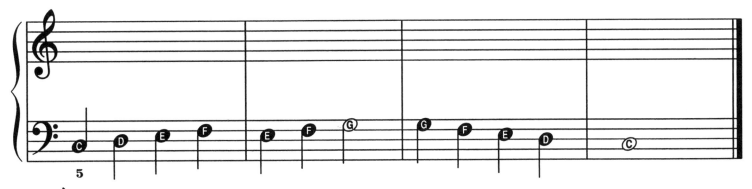

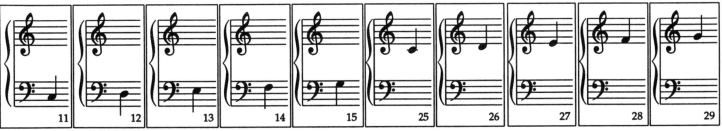

 The use of flashcards is highly recommended to aid in recognizing individual notes. *Music Flashcards* (GP27) by Jane Smisor Bastien may be obtained from your local music dealer. Each flashcard is numbered. Find the numbered cards shown below from your set of music flashcards. Name, play, and memorize these new notes.

Rest Signs

Rest signs in music indicate measured silence. There is a rest sign with the same value as each note.

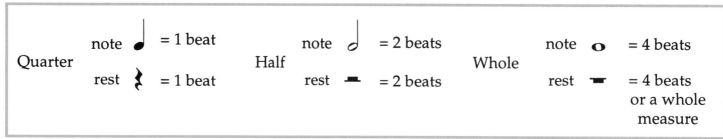

	note	= 1 beat		note	= 2 beats		note	= 4 beats
Quarter			Half			Whole		
	rest	= 1 beat		rest	= 2 beats		rest	= 4 beats or a whole measure

MOVING ALONG

DISC ONE ⑨ ♩ = 96

quarter rest   half rest

whole rest

JINGLE BELLS

DISC ONE ⑩ ♩ = 120

Words and Music by
James S. Pierpont

Jin - gle bells,   jin - gle bells,   jin - gle all the   way.

Oh, what fun it   is to ride a   one horse o - pen   sleigh!

More About Clefs

- The **Treble Clef** sign is also known as the **G Clef Sign.**

- The Treble Clef sign wraps around the 2nd line.
  The 2nd line indicates the note **G.**

- The **Bass Clef** sign is also known as the **F Clef Sign.**

- The dots of the Bass Clef sign surround the 4th line on the staff.
  The 4th line indicates the note **F.**

- It is helpful to use these reference points to recognize notes.

Note Review

Write the letter names of the notes in the blanks.

Trace the
Treble Clef
Sign.

1. ____   2. ____   3. ____   4. ____   5. ____   6. ____

Trace the
Bass Clef
Sign.

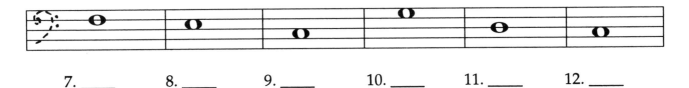

7. ____   8. ____   9. ____   10. ____   11. ____   12. ____

Draw a
Treble Clef
Sign.

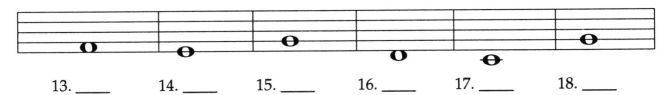

13. ____   14. ____   15. ____   16. ____   17. ____   18. ____

Draw a
Bass Clef
Sign.

19. ____   20. ____   21. ____   22. ____   23. ____   24. ____

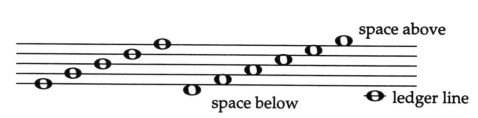

Review

Use the staff example shown to help answer the following questions.

space above

space below   ◯ ledger line

A. What is the name of the note on the:

1. 3rd line  _____

2. 1st line  _____

3. 2nd line 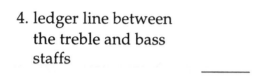 _____

4. ledger line between the treble and bass staffs

_____

5. 4th line  _____

B. What is the name of the note in the:

1. 1st space  _____

2. space below _____

3. 3rd space  _____

4. 2nd space _____

5. 4th space  _____

C. Write the number of beats each rest or note receives in $\frac{4}{4}$.

1. _____ 2. _____ 3. _____ 4. _____ 5. _____ 6. _____ 7. _____

D. Add bar lines to divide the rhythm into measures.

E. Add one note to complete each measure.

F. Add one rest to complete each measure.

KP1

Melodic and Harmonic Intervals: 2nds and 3rds

- ◆ The distance between two notes is called an **interval**.
- ◆ **Melodic** intervals consist of notes played one at a time to form a melody (tune).
- ◆ **Harmonic** intervals consist of notes played simultaneously to form harmony.

On the keyboard:
- ◆ **Neighbor white keys** are a 2nd apart.
- ◆ A 3rd **skips** a white key.

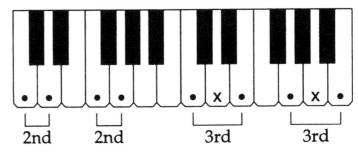

On the staff:
A **2nd** is written from a **line to the next space**   OR   a **2nd** is written from a **space to the next line**.

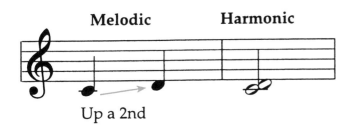

On the staff:
A **3rd** is written from a **line to the next line**   OR   a **3rd** is written from a **space to the next space**.

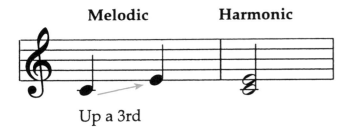

INTERVAL ETUDE

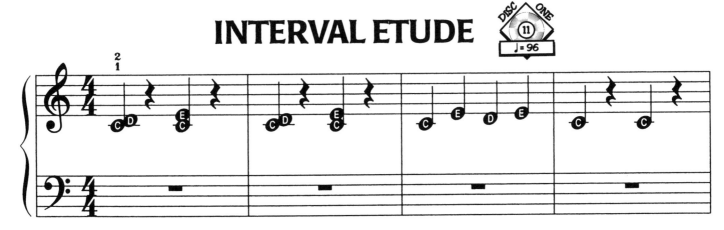

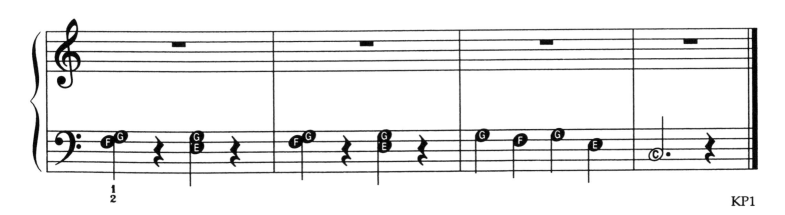

Dynamic Signs

Dynamic signs in music indicate how loudly or softly to play.

SIGN	ITALIAN NAME	MEANING
p	*piano*	soft
mp	*mezzo piano*	medium soft
mf	*mezzo forte*	medium loud
f	*forte*	loud

Write the names of the intervals (2nd or 3rd) in the boxes provided.

KP1

Tied Notes

A **tie** is a curved line which connects notes on the **same** line or space. Play the first note only and hold for the value of both notes.

Hold, do not play again.

Count: 1 2 3 4   1 2 3 4

ALL THROUGH THE NIGHT

R.H. 4 begins on ____.
L.H. 2 begins on ____.

Welsh Lullaby

Sleep,   my   child,   and   peace   at - tend   thee,

All   through   the   night. _____

Guard - ian   an - gels,   God   will   send   thee,

All   through   the   night. _____

Review

A. Draw arrows (up or down) and write the names of the intervals (2nd or 3rd) in the boxes provided.
B. Write the letter names of the notes in the blanks.
C. Play these notes in the correct place on the keyboard.

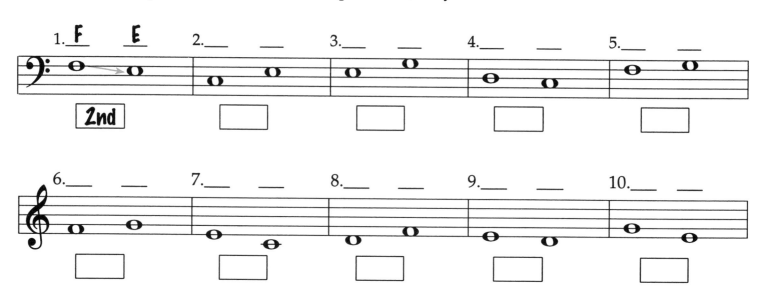

D. Write the names of the intervals (2nd or 3rd) in the boxes provided.
E. Write the letter names of the notes in the blanks.
F. Play these notes in the correct place on the keyboard.

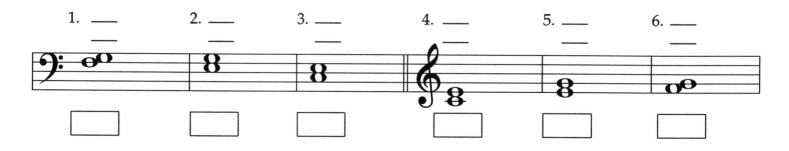

G. Draw notes up or down from the given notes to form the indicated **melodic** intervals.
H. Write the letter names of the notes in the blanks.
I. Play these notes in the correct place on the keyboard.

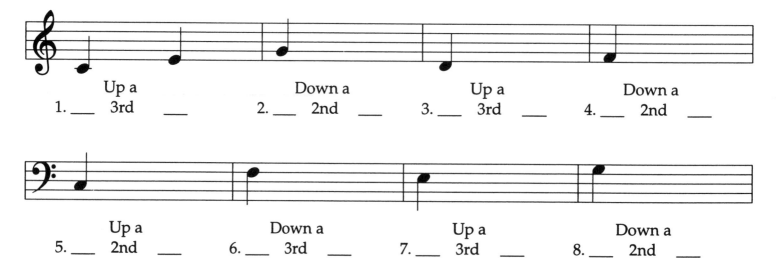

Melodic and Harmonic Intervals: 4ths and 5ths

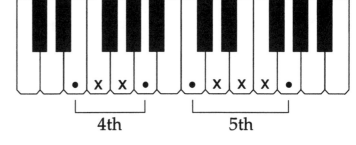

On the keyboard:
- A **4th skips two** white keys.

- A **5th skips three** white keys.

4th   5th

On the staff:

A **4th** is written from a **line to a space**   OR   a **4th** is written from a **space to a line**.

Melodic	Harmonic

Up a 4th

Melodic	Harmonic

Down a 4th

On the staff:

A **5th** is written from a **line to a line**   OR   a **5th** is written from a **space to a space**.

Melodic	Harmonic

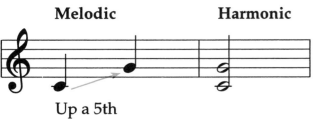

Up a 5th

Melodic	Harmonic

Down a 5th

INTERVAL WORKOUT

R.H. 1 begins on ____.
L.H. 1 begins on ____.

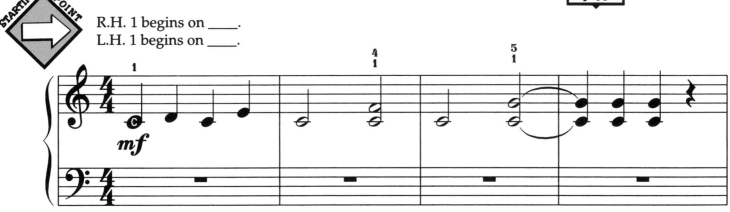

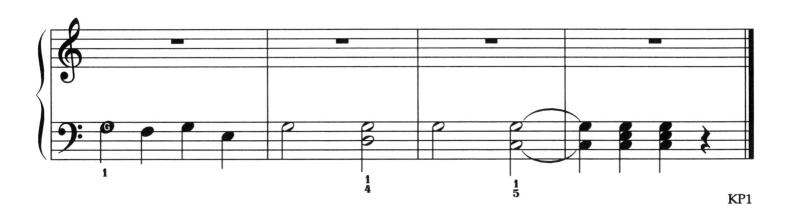

KP1

Richard Wagner (1813 - 1883), German composer, was fifteen when he heard *Symphony No. 9* by Beethoven and decided to become a composer. He began writing operas in the German Romantic style. As his career progressed, Wagner's operas evolved into musical dramas and he revolutionized opera as an art form. To create drama, he greatly enlarged the orchestra, expanded the instrumentation, and created new and exciting harmonies. Wagner wrote his own opera *librettos* (words), basing his mature works on history and medieval myths and legends. In addition, he used highly dramatic and powerful singers and *leitmotifs* (short descriptive tunes) to describe characters. Wagner strove to merge the different arts: poetry, dance, music, and painting, into one extraordinary unified art work through a new synthesis of music and drama. The *Bridal March* excerpt below is from Wagner's famous opera *Lohengrin*. Franz Liszt conducted the first performance of *Lohengrin* at Weimar in 1850.

BRIDAL MARCH

R.H. 1 begins on ____.
L.H. 5 begins on ____.

Richard Wagner

STAR GAZING

R.H. 1 begins on ____.
L.H. 1 begins on ____.

Slur

A **slur** is a curved line over or under two or more different notes that are to be played **legato** (smooth, connected). The slur is used to show a musical thought called a **phrase**. Lift your hand at the end of each slur by rolling the wrist forward and upward in a relaxed and gentle manner.

AURA LEE

L.H. 5 begins on ____.
R.H. 1 begins on ____.

George R. Poulton

MARCHING ON MAIN STREET

L.H. 1 begins on ____.
R.H. 5 begins on ____.

KP1

Review

A. Draw arrows (up or down) and write the names of the intervals (4th or 5th) in the boxes provided.
B. Write the letter names of the notes in the blanks.
C. Play these notes in the correct place on the keyboard.

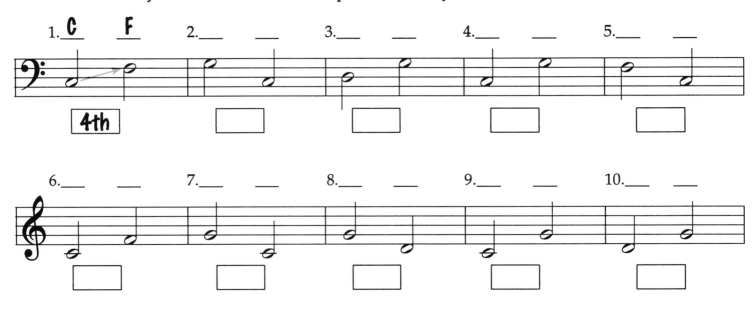

D. Write the names of the intervals (4th or 5th) in the boxes provided.
E. Write the letter names of the notes in the blanks.
F. Play these notes in the correct place on the keyboard.

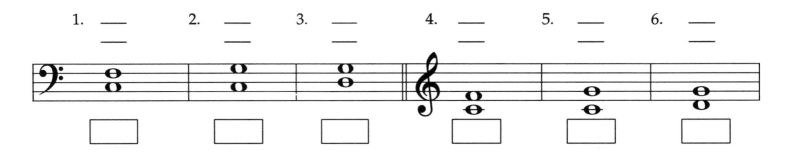

G. Draw notes up or down from the given notes to form the indicated **melodic** intervals.
H. Write the letter names of the notes in the blanks.
I. Play these notes in the correct place on the keyboard.

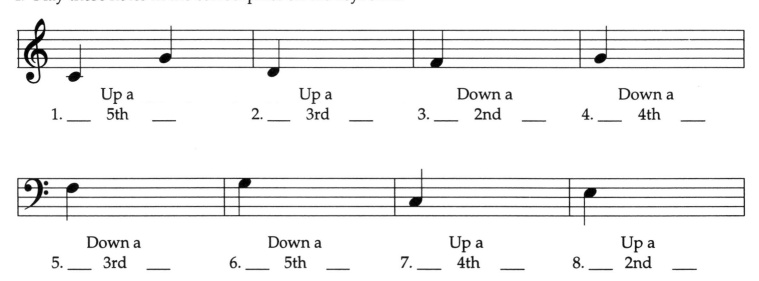

Challenge Piece

A "Challenge Piece" is included at the end of every chapter. These pieces offer a variety of challenges to help improve your piano skills.

$\frac{3}{4}$ = 3 beats in a measure.
= ♩ receives 1 beat.
♩ receives 2 beats.
♩. receives 3 beats.

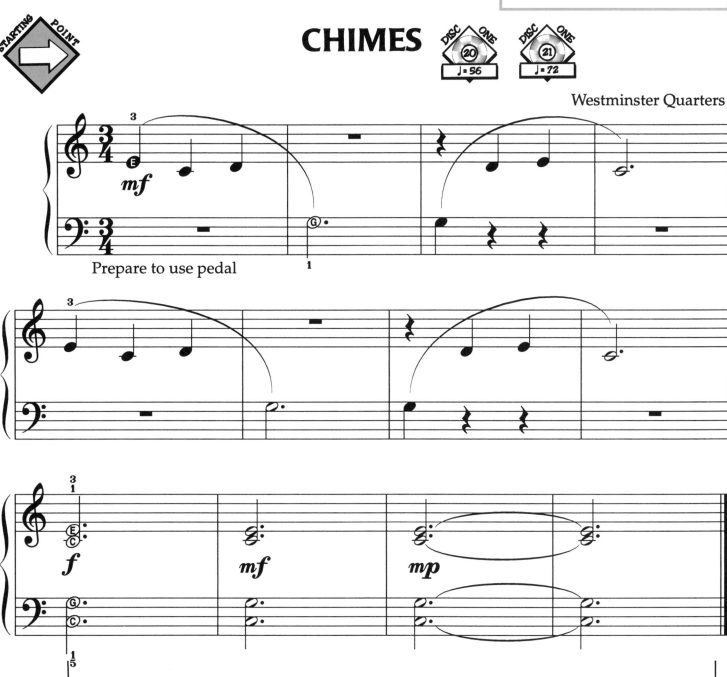

CHIMES

Westminster Quarters

Prepare to use pedal

Press pedal and hold

Release Pedal

Damper Pedal

The damper pedal (on the right) is used to sustain tones. When pressed, the dampers lift from the strings to allow the strings to vibrate freely. This sign ⌐___⌐ indicates when to use the damper pedal. Before you begin to play, put the ball of your foot on the pedal and keep your heel on the floor. Your heel should always remain in contact with the floor.

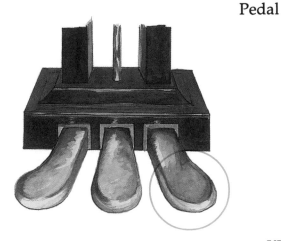

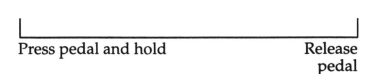

Press pedal and hold   Release pedal

Review

A. Write the letter names of the notes in the blanks.
B. Play these notes in the correct place on the keyboard.

1. ____ 2. ____ 3. ____ 4. ____ 5. ____ 6. ____

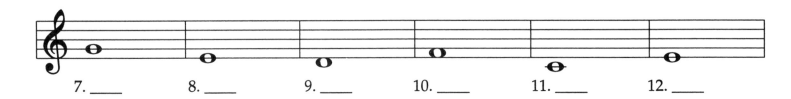

7. ____ 8. ____ 9. ____ 10. ____ 11. ____ 12. ____

13. ____ 14. ____ 15. ____ 16. ____ 17. ____ 18. ____

C. Draw arrows up or down and write the names of the intervals (2nd, 3rd, 4th, or 5th) in the boxes provided.
D. Write the letter names of the notes in the blanks.
E. Play these notes in the correct place on the keyboard.

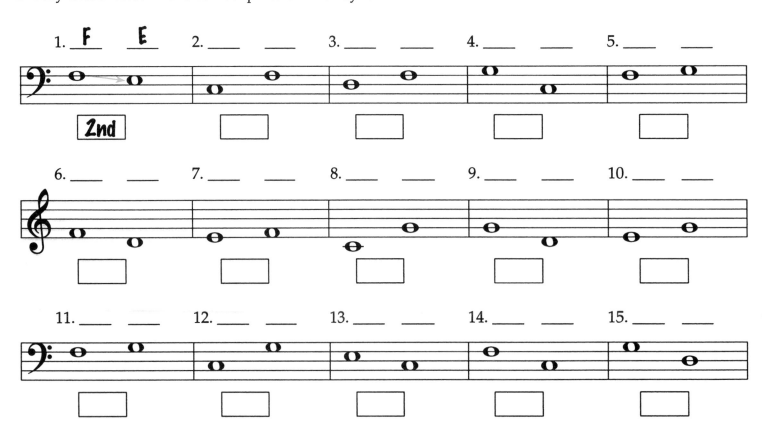

1. **F** **E** 2. ____ ____ 3. ____ ____ 4. ____ ____ 5. ____ ____

2nd

6. ____ ____ 7. ____ ____ 8. ____ ____ 9. ____ ____ 10. ____ ____

11. ____ ____ 12. ____ ____ 13. ____ ____ 14. ____ ____ 15. ____ ____

F. Write the number of beats each rest and note receives in $\frac{4}{4}$.

1. _____ 2. _____ 3. _____ 4. _____ 5. _____ 6. _____ 7. _____

G. Add bar lines to divide the rhythm into measures.

H. Add one note to complete each measure.

I. Add one rest to complete each measure.

J. Identify the following as a slur or a tie.

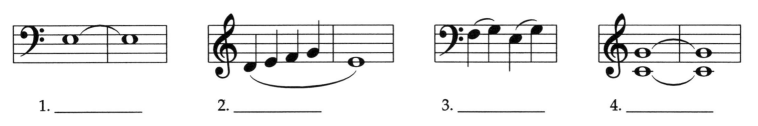

1. _____ 2. _____ 3. _____ 4. _____

K. Identify the following dynamic markings.

1. $\boldsymbol{f}$ = ___forte___ = ___loud___   3. $\boldsymbol{mp}$ = _____ = _____
        Italian   *English*   *Italian*   *English*

2. $\boldsymbol{mf}$ = _____ = _____   4. $\boldsymbol{p}$ = _____ = _____
        Italian   *English*   *Italian*   *English*

Chapter 3
Harmonizing Melodies

- ◆ The Flat Sign ♭
- ◆ Chord symbols
- ◆ Harmonizing melodies with C, G7, and F chords
- ◆ Upbeat
- ◆ Fermata

More about the C Chord

Roman numerals are used to name tones or **degrees** within each key.

In the Key of C:

- ◆ The C chord is built on **Degree I** which is C.
- ◆ C is called the **tonic note**, or **key note**.
- ◆ A **chord** built on the tonic note is called a **tonic chord** or a **I chord**.
- ◆ The **root** is the note from which a chord originates. The root of the C chord is C.

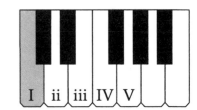

C Chord = Tonic Chord = I Chord

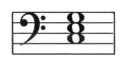

CHORD PRELUDE

L.H. 5 begins on ____.
R.H. 1 begins on ____.

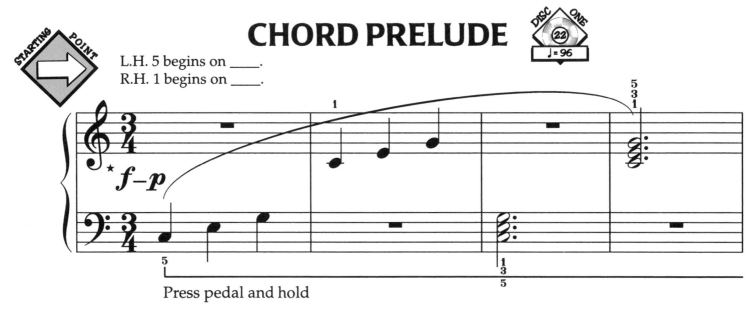

Press pedal and hold

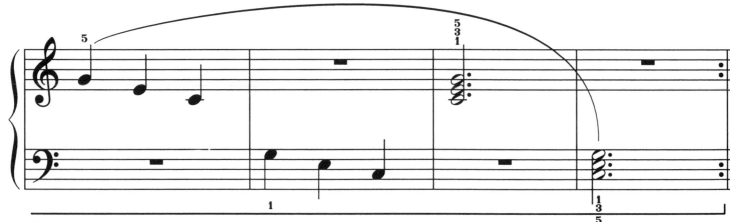

★ *f–p* means to play the first time *forte* and the second time *piano*.

Release pedal

Balancing Melody and Accompaniment

Chords are often used to form the accompaniment for melodies. The melody should always sing above the accompaniment . To achieve a good sound, balance your hands by playing the melody louder and the chords softer.

ROUND AND ROUND

L.H. 1 begins on _____.
R.H. begins on a _____ chord.

L.H. melody

BELLS IN THE DISTANCE

R.H. 3 begins on _____.
L.H. begins on a _____ chord.

Moving to the G7 Chord

In the C 5-Finger Position:

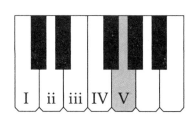
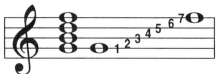

- ◆ The G7 chord is built on **Degree V** which is G.
- ◆ **G** is called the **dominant note**.
- ◆ A G7 chord is also called a **dominant 7th chord** or a **V7 chord**.
- ◆ There are 4 notes in the complete G7 chord: **G B D F**
- ◆ **G** is the **root** of the G7 chord.
- ◆ The number 7 means that F is 7 tones above G.
- ◆ For ease in accompanying at the introductory level, you will play a G7 chord made up of 3 notes in the arrangement shown below:

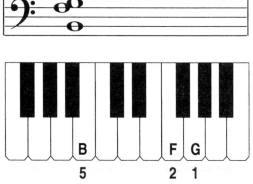
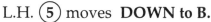

L.H. ⑤ moves **DOWN** to B.

R.H. ① moves **DOWN** to B.

CHORD ETUDE

L.H. 5 begins on ____.
R.H. 1 begins on ____.

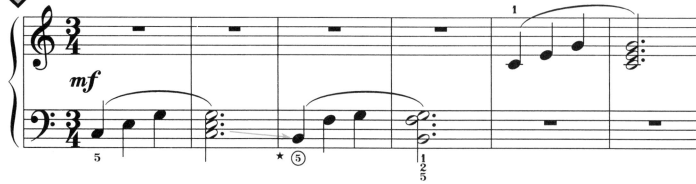

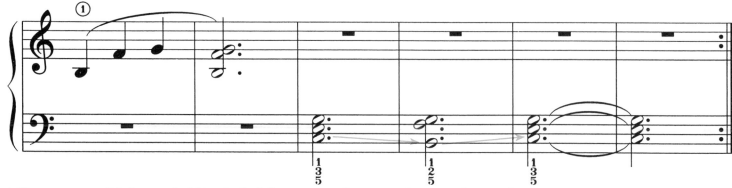

★ From pages 34 through 111, circled finger numbers are frequently used to indicate a finger or hand position change.

Find the numbered cards shown from your set of *Music Flashcards*. Name, play, and memorize these notes.

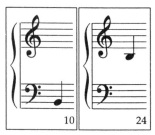

KP1

Chord Progressions and Chord Symbols

A **Chord Progression** consists of two or more chords played consecutively. The **I** and **V7** chords are used in many chord progressions to harmonize melodies. **Chord Symbols** name specific chords. A letter placed over a note indicates a chord that could be played with that note. You will see a new chord symbol each time a chord change occurs. Chord symbols are often placed **above** the treble staff in popular music. The chord symbol for the **C** chord is **C**. The chord symbol for the **G7** chord is **G7**.

GOODNIGHT, LADIES

Words and Music by
E.P. Christy

STARTING POINT
R.H. 3 begins on ____.
L.H. 1 begins on ____.

KP1

WARM UP

PROMENADE

R.H. 5 begins on ____.
L.H. 1 begins on ____.

ROW, ROW, ROW YOUR BOAT

L.H. 5 begins on ____.
R.H. 1 begins on ____.

Traditional Round

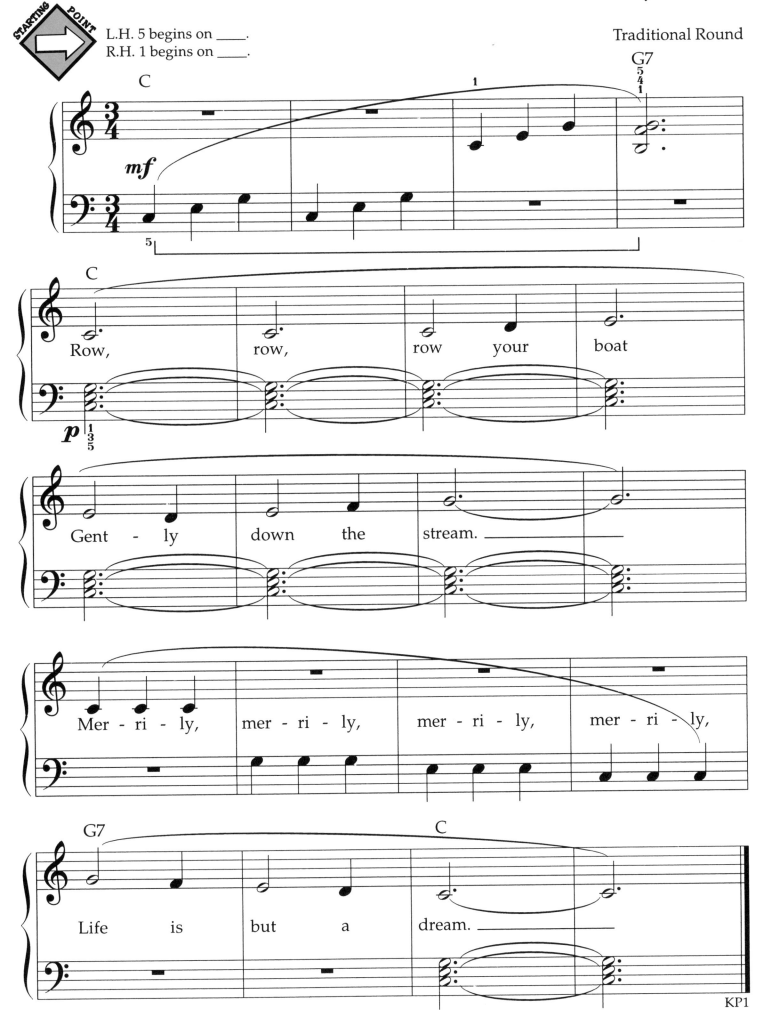

Row, row, row your boat

Gent - ly down the stream.

Mer - ri - ly, mer - ri - ly, mer - ri - ly, mer - ri - ly,

Life is but a dream.

KP1

38

Review

A. In the C 5-Finger position:
    1. The tonic note is _____.
    2. The dominant note is _____.
B. Write chord symbols (C,G7) in the boxes provided.
C. Play this example in the correct place on the keyboard.

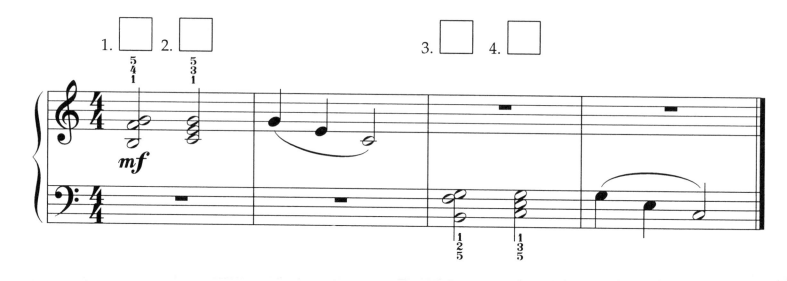

Note: The notes of a chord are often divided between the hands. In *Peaceful Dreams*, the L.H. plays C and G together while the R.H. plays E.

PEACEFUL DREAMS

R.H. 3 begins on ____.
L.H. 1 begins on ____.
L.H. 5 begins on ____.

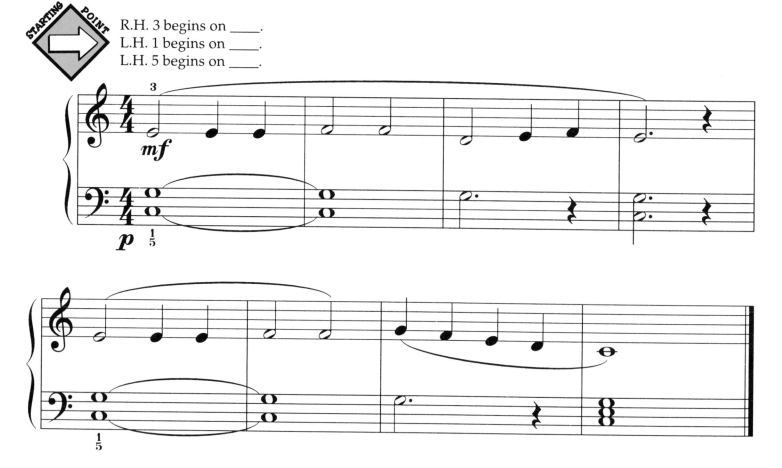

Upbeat

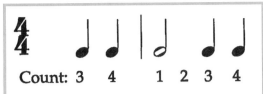

Count: 3 4 1 2 3 4

Notes that come before the first full measure of a piece are called **upbeats**. Usually, the time value of the upbeats is taken away from the final measure, making the final measure incomplete. The beats in the first measure plus the beats in the last measure equal one full measure.

SIMPLE GIFTS

L.H. 1 begins on ____.
R.H. 1 begins on ____.

Shaker melody

KP1

Moving to the F Chord

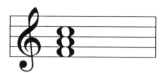
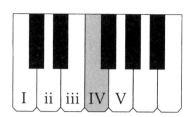

In the C 5-Finger Position:

◆ The **F chord** is built on **Degree IV** which is **F**.

◆ F is called the **subdominant note**.

◆ The F chord is also called a **subdominant chord**, or a **IV Chord**.

◆ There are 3 notes in the F chord: **F A C**

◆ **F** is the **root** of the F chord.

◆ For ease in accompanying at the introductory level, you will play an F chord in the arrangement shown below:

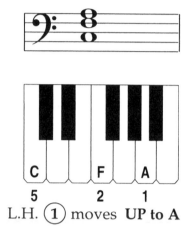

L.H. ① moves **UP to A**

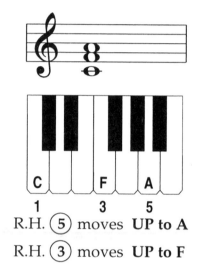

R.H. ⑤ moves **UP to A**

R.H. ③ moves **UP to F**

L.H. 5 begins on ____.
R.H. 1 begins on ____.

CHORD ETUDE

Find the numbered cards shown from your set of *Music Flashcards*. Name, play, and memorize these notes.

WARM UP

KUM BA YAH

L.H. 5 begins on ____.
R.H. begins on a ____ chord.

African Spiritual

WARM UP

FANFARE

R.H. 1 begins on ____.
L.H. 5 begins on ____.

Fermata Sign

A fermata sign indicates a pause in music. Hold the note or notes under a fermata sign longer than their original time value.

1. Write the chord symbols (C or F) in the boxes provided.
2. Begin by playing hands separately, naming the L.H. melody notes aloud as you play.
3. Play hands together, counting aloud.

FOR HE'S A JOLLY GOOD FELLOW

L.H. 5 begins on _____.
R.H. begins on a _____ chord.

Traditional English Song

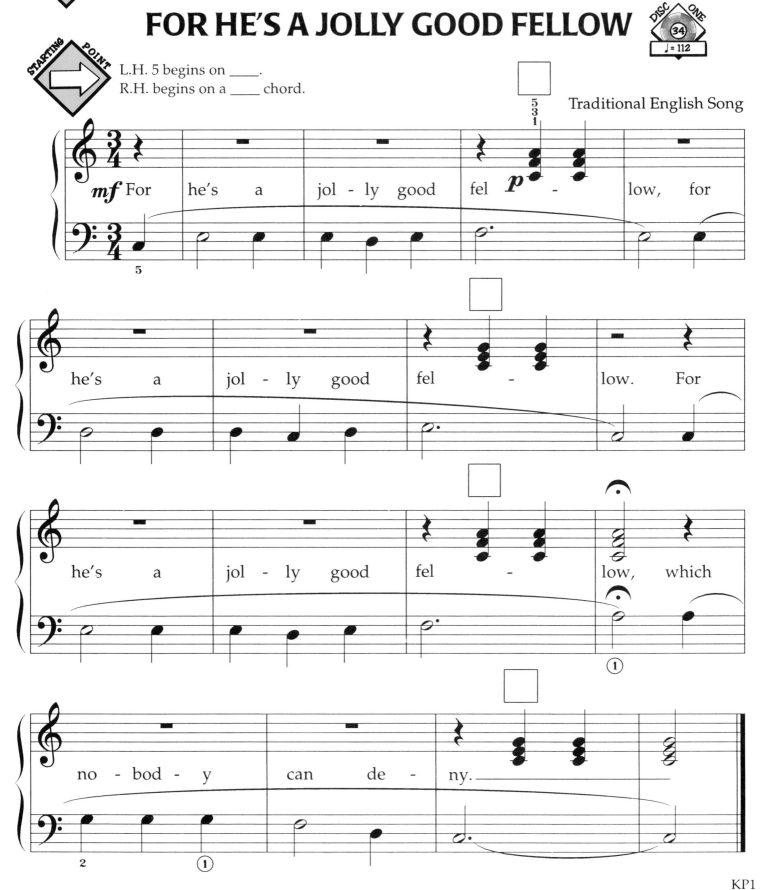

WHEN THE SAINTS GO MARCHING IN

R.H. 1 begins on ____.
L.H. 5 begins on ____.

Traditional African-American Song

KP1

Challenge Piece

Flat Sign ♭

A **flat sign** ♭ before a note means to play the nearest key to the **left**.
The nearest key may be a black or white key.

A flat note remains flat for the whole measure.

(also G♭'s)   (also E♭'s)

PERSIAN MARKET

R.H. 1 begins on ____.
L.H. 2 begins on ____.

also D♭

★ The term *dim.* (an abbreviation for the word *diminuendo*) means to gradually play softer; *rit.* (an abbreviation for the word *ritardando*) means to gradually slow down; the letter *"e"* means "and." KP1

Review

A. Draw X's on the keyboards to indicate the given notes.

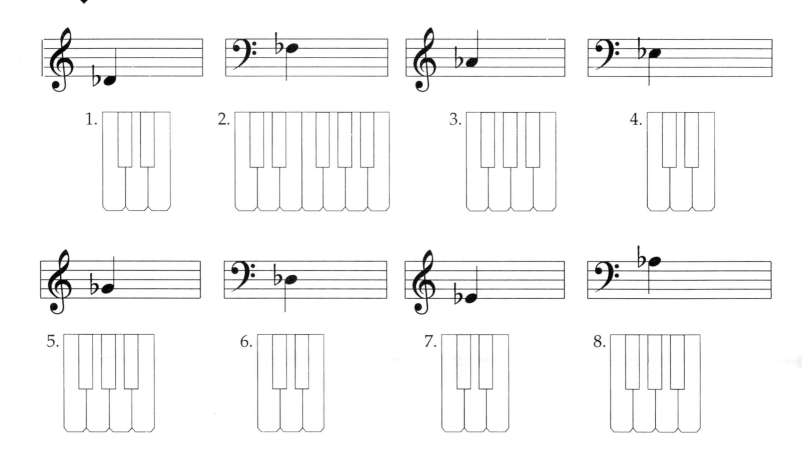

B. Draw a flat sign before each note that has a flat written above or below it.
C. Write the names of the flat notes in the blanks.
D. Play and name the notes aloud.

The "round" part of the flat is centered:

on a line　　　or　　　in a space

E. Write the names of the intervals (2nd, 3rd, 4th, or 5th) in the boxes provided.
F. Write the letter names of the notes in the blanks.
G. Play the notes in the correct place on the keyboard.

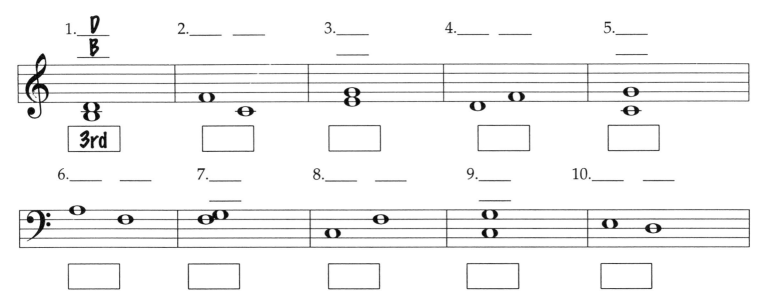

H. Write the chord symbols (C, G7, F) in the boxes provided.
I. Play the chords in the correct place on the keyboard.

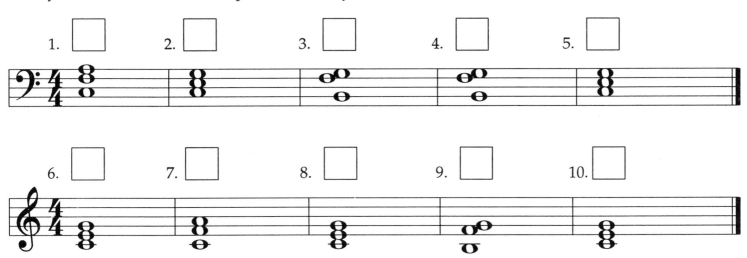

J. Harmonize
   When playing *Hot Cross Buns*, add L.H. chords by following the chord symbols given.

Chapter 4
Reading in Middle C

- ◆ 1st and 2nd endings
- ◆ Sharp Sign ♯
- ◆ Tempo marks
- ◆ Eighth notes ♫
- ◆ Staccato touch
- ◆ *8va* sign

Middle C Position

Middle C is played with:
- ◆ R.H. if the stem is up.
- ◆ L.H. if the stem is down.

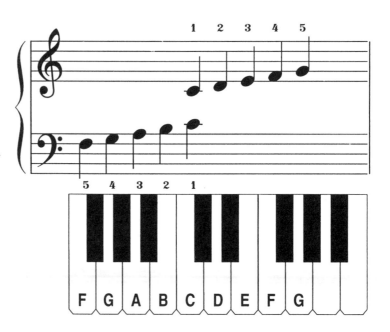

MIDDLE C PRELUDE

L.H. 5 begins on ____.
R.H. 1 begins on ____.

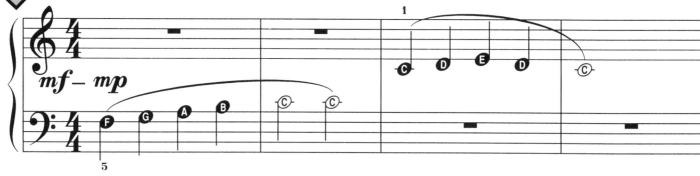

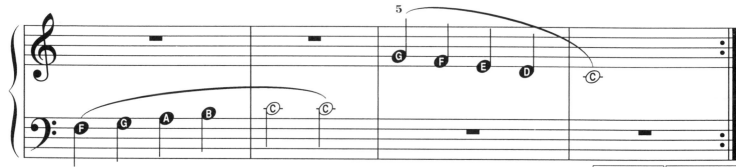

Find the numbered cards shown from your set of *Music Flashcards*.
Name, play, and memorize these notes.

KP1

Tempo Marks

Tempo Marks are placed at the beginning of a piece to tell the rate of speed at which a piece is to be played. Tempo marks are usually in Italian. The most common tempo marks are:

Andante	Slowly, walking tempo	**Allegretto**	Moderately fast
Moderato	Moderately	**Allegro**	Fast

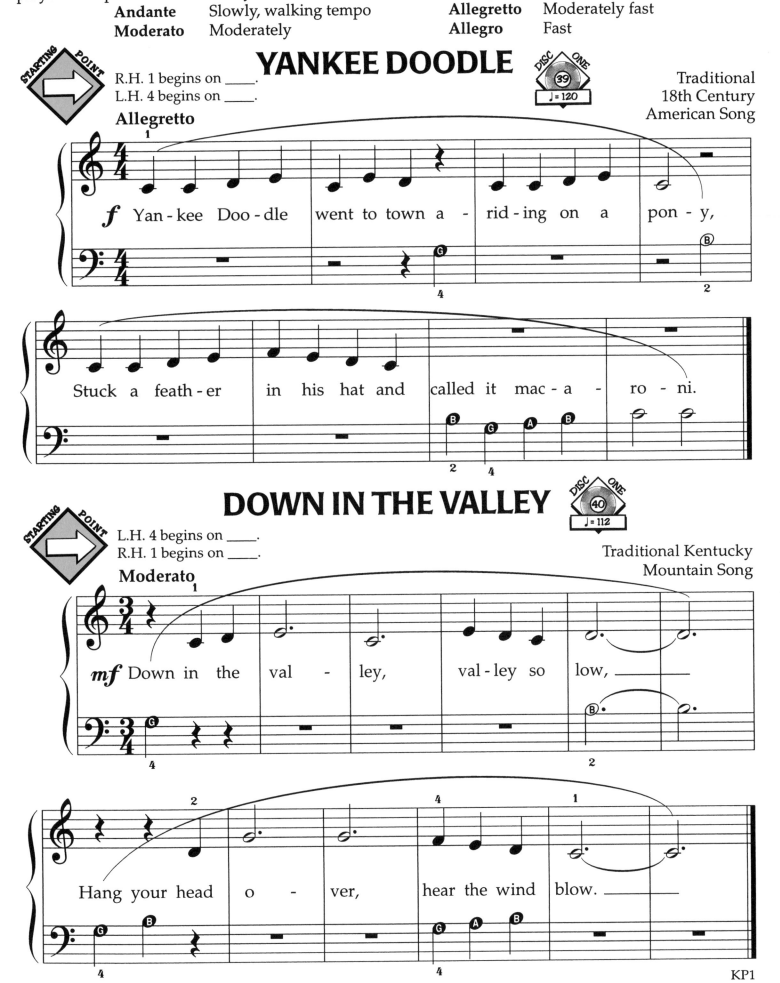

Review

A. Draw arrows (up or down) and write the names of the intervals (2nd, 3rd, 4th, or 5th) in the boxes provided.
B. Write the letter names of the notes in the blanks.
C. Play these notes in the correct place on the keyboard.

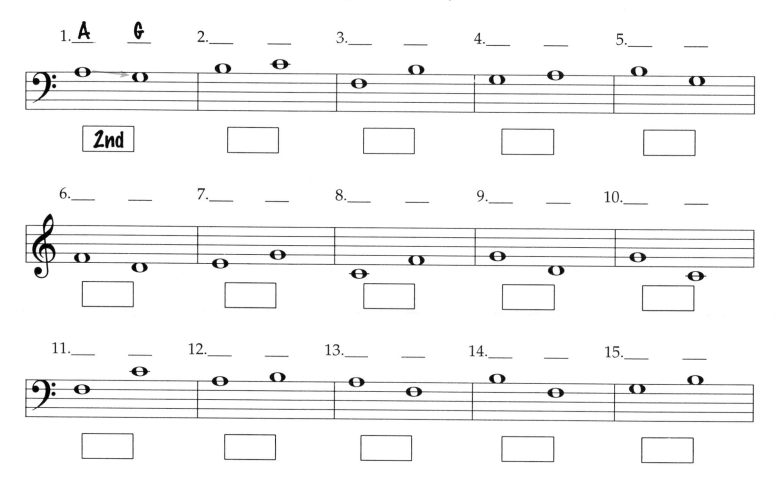

1. <u>A</u>   <u>G</u>   2.___ ___   3.___ ___   4.___ ___   5.___ ___

2nd

6.___ ___   7.___ ___   8.___ ___   9.___ ___   10.___ ___

11.___ ___   12.___ ___   13.___ ___   14.___ ___   15.___ ___

D. Draw notes up or down from the given notes to form the indicated intervals.
E. Write the letter names of the notes in the blanks.
F. Play these notes in the correct place on the keyboard.

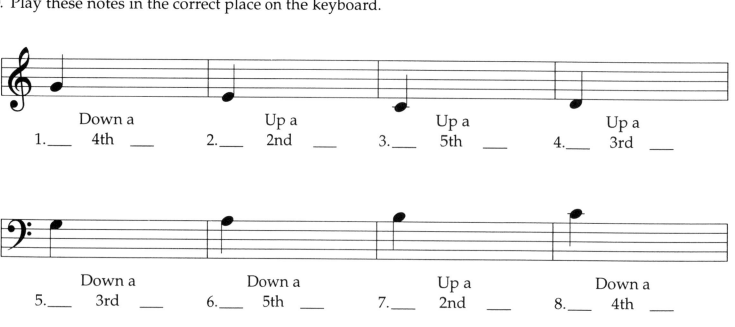

Down a
1.___ 4th ___

Up a
2.___ 2nd ___

Up a
3.___ 5th ___

Up a
4.___ 3rd ___

Down a
5.___ 3rd ___

Down a
6.___ 5th ___

Up a
7.___ 2nd ___

Down a
8.___ 4th ___

Sharp Sign ♯

A **sharp sign** ♯ before a note means to play the nearest key to the **right**.
The nearest key may be a black or white key.

A sharp note remains sharp for the whole measure.

(also F ♯)

CAN CAN
from the opera *Orpheus in the Underworld*

Jacques Offenbach

Frédéric Chopin (1810-1849), Polish composer, became the favorite French *salon* player of the 1830's in Paris. Chopin specialized in composing works for the piano; almost all of his work is for solo piano. He created masterpiece after masterpiece and was his own worst critic. French novelist Georges Sand (Madame Dudevant) described Chopin's composing "state" as follows: "He analyzed very much when writing down what was conceived as a whole, and his regret that he could not represent it perfectly made him desperate. For days, he locked himself up in his room, running up and down, breaking pens, repeating, changing one single measure a hundred times, writing, scratching it out, and the next morning starting all over again with painstaking and desperate efforts. He would work six weeks on one single page . . ." *(Milton Cross' Encyclopedia Of The Great Composers And Their Music)*. Chopin's works include concertos, polonaises, waltzes, etudes, mazurkas, ballades, scherzos, preludes, nocturnes, and others. The following excerpt is from Chopin's famous *Fantaisie Impromptu*.

A **flat sign** ♭ before a note means to play the next key to the **left**.

A **sharp sign** ♯ before a note means to play the next key to the **right**.

FANTAISIE IMPROMPTU

Frédéric Chopin

Review

A. Draw X's on the keyboards to indicate the given notes.

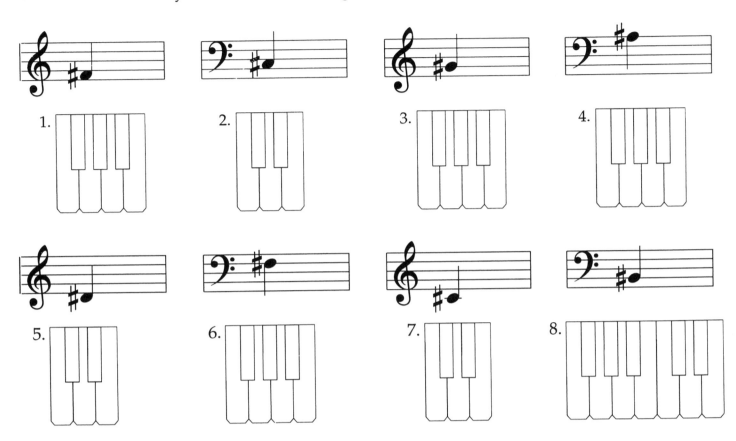

B. Draw a sharp sign before each note that has a sharp (♯) over or under it.
C. Write the names of the sharp notes in the blanks.
D. Play and name the notes aloud.

The "square" part of the sharp is centered:

on a **line**   or   in a **space.**

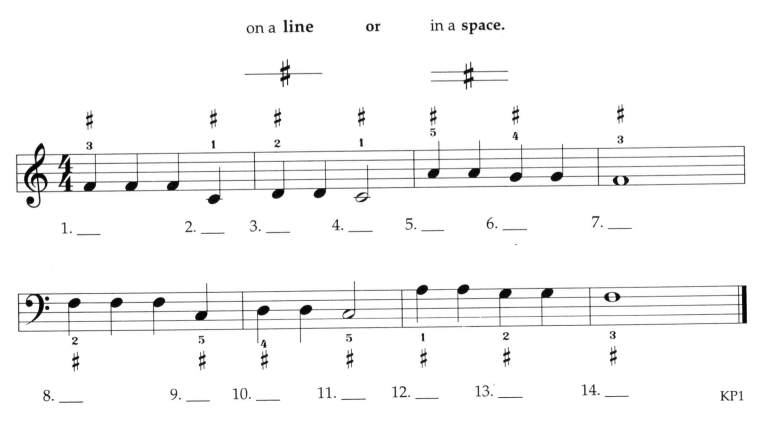

KP1

Two Eighth Notes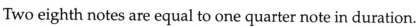

Two eighth notes are equal to one quarter note in duration.  = 1 beat
Two eighth notes are paired together with a beam.
To count eighth notes, it is helpful to subdivide each single beat into two parts.

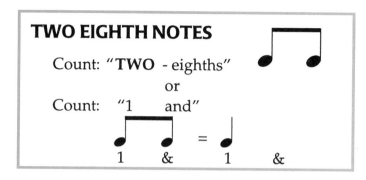

TWO EIGHTH NOTES

Count: "**TWO** - eighths"

or

Count: "1 and"

1 & = 1 &

Clap and count to the following rhythm aloud.

3 & | 1 & 2 & 3 & | 1 & 2 & 3 & | 1 & 2 & 3 & | 1 & 2 &

Count aloud: 3   and | 1 and 2 and...

 Write the counts in the music.

ANOTHER YEAR OLDER?

L.H. 4 begins on ____.
R.H. 1 begins on ____.

Moderato

Johann Sebastian Bach (1685 - 1750), German composer, was the musical director to several royal courts where his duties included writing music for church services and for special events such as weddings and funerals. Bach wrote an extraordinary amount of music including chorale preludes, cantatas, keyboard music such as *The Well Tempered Clavier*, sonatas for various instruments, orchestral pieces such as the *Brandenburg Concertos*, the *Mass in B Minor*, and many others. Today, Bach is considered to be one of the most gifted figures in the history of music. During his lifetime however, he was highly respected more as an organ player and organ technician than as a composer. The excerpt below from Bach's *Minuet in G* is part of the collection entitled *Notebook for Anna Magdelena Bach*. Anna Magdelena was Bach's second wife. On her twenty-fifth birthday, he gave her a notebook containing pieces for the members of his family to play.

1st and 2nd Endings

In order to save space, 1st and 2nd endings are used when a portion of a piece is repeated.

1.   Return to the beginning and repeat.

2.   After repeating the 1st section, skip the measures within the 1st ending and go directly to the 2nd ending.

R.H. 2 begins on ____.
L.H. 4 begins on ____.

MINUET IN G

Johann Sebastian Bach

KP1

Review

A. Write the number of beats each note or rest receives in $\frac{4}{4}$.

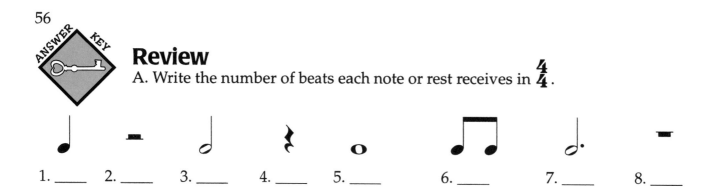

1. ____   2. ____   3. ____   4. ____   5. ____   6. ____   7. ____   8. ____

B. Add bar lines to complete each measure.

C. Add one note to complete each measure.

D. Add one rest to complete each measure.

E. Write the chord symbols (C, G7, F) in the boxes provided.
F. Play the chords in the correct place on the keyboard.

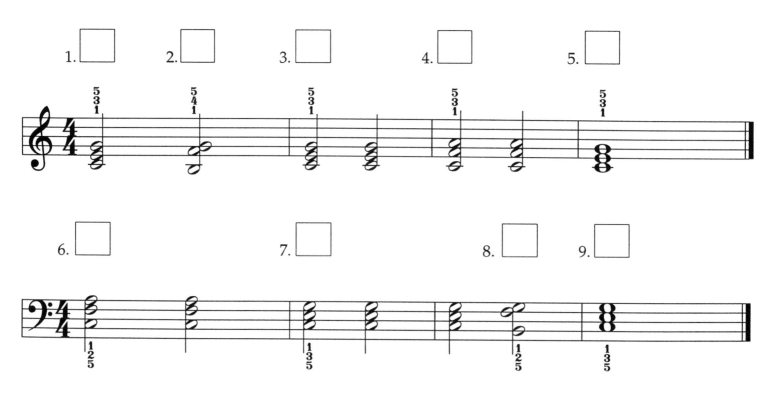

KP1

Octave Sign *8va*

When the sign *8va* is placed over a note(s), play the note(s) one octave (eight notes) higher than written.
When the sign *8va* is placed under a note(s), play the note(s) one octave lower than written.

EARLY MORNING STROLL

Staccato ♪

Staccato means to play in a short or detached manner by releasing a key immediately after playing.
A dot over or under a note indicates to play staccato.

FOOTSTEPS IN THE NIGHT

 L.H. 4 begins on _____.
R.H. 2 begins on _____.

Moderato

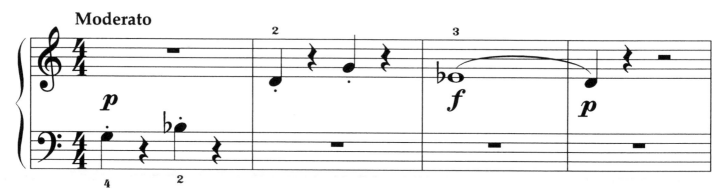

Franz Joseph Haydn (1732 - 1809), Austrian composer, was extremely important in the development of the symphony, sonata, and string quartet. He expanded the outlines of these forms, experimented with orchestrations and harmonies, added new instruments to the symphonic ensemble, created unprecedented lyrical and expressive melodies, and helped to form the symphonic ensemble as we know it today. The excerpt below is taken from the second movement of *Symphony No. 94 in G Major*, better known as *Surprise Symphony*. This movement begins with a soft and placid theme only to be interrupted without warning by a loud "surprise" chord for full orchestra. Legend has it that Haydn placed this "surprise" chord in the slow movement to wake up the audience members.

SURPRISE SYMPHONY

R.H. 1 begins on ____.
L.H. 2 begins on ____.

Franz Joseph Haydn

Technic

Technical exercises are designed to help develop hand and finger coordination, and to develop ease, control, and facility at the keyboard. Throughout the remainder of this book, use the technic exercises in each chapter as a warm up to your daily practice.

Practice Suggestions

1. Playing and counting aloud with a metronome will help ensure a steady tempo. Play this piece three times a day, using three different tempos:

   Slow (♩ = 60)   Medium (♩ = 72)   Fast (♩ = 96)

2. Play using the correct articulation marks; some notes are staccato and some are legato.
3. Focus on forming a good hand position with a relaxed wrist.

JUMP AND GLIDE

L.H. 5 begins on _____.
R.H. 1 begins on _____.

Challenge Piece

When the melody is in the L.H., the R.H. chords are played softer.
All dotted half notes 𝅗𝅥. receive 3 full beats.

WALTZ FOR THE LEFT HAND

L.H. 3 begins on _____.
R.H. begins on a _____ chord.

Andante

Review

A. Write the names of the intervals (2nd, 3rd, 4th, or 5th) in the boxes provided.
B. Write the letter names of the notes in the blanks.
C. Play the notes in the correct place on the keyboard.

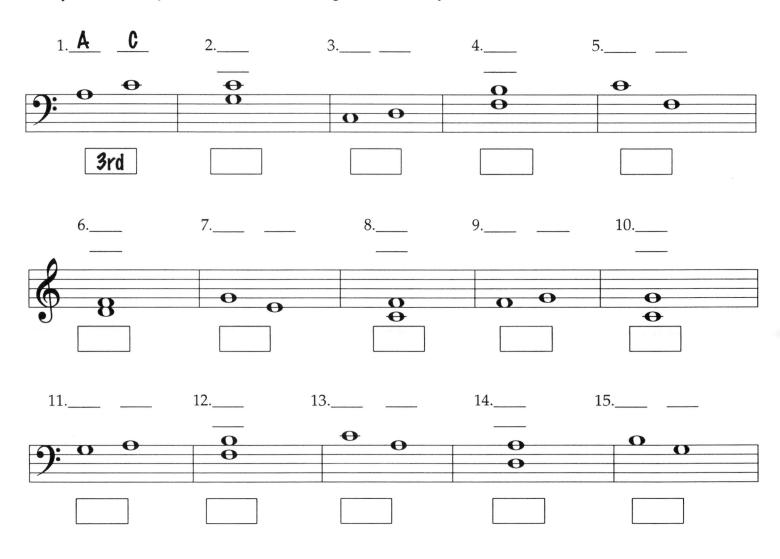

D. Write the chord symbols (C, G7, F) in the boxes provided.
E. Play the chords in the correct place on the keyboard.

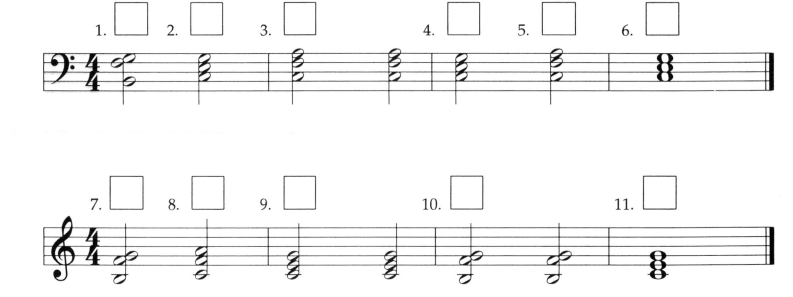

F. Add one note to complete each measure.

G. Draw X's on the keyboards to indicate the given notes.

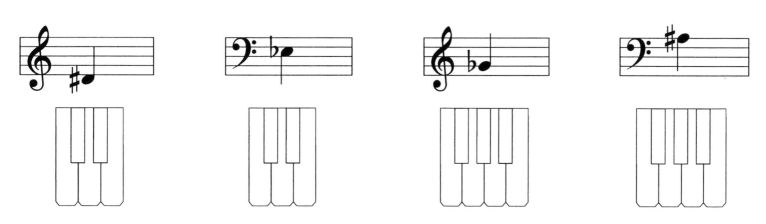

H. Match each music example to its correct definition.

a.

_____ Play one octave higher than written

b.

_____ Play short, detached.

_____ The symbol indicating to play the next key to the right.

c.

_____ The symbol indicating to play the next key to the left.

d. ♭

Chapter 5
Reading in G

◆ Reading in the Key of G	◆ Key Signature
◆ Time Signature $\frac{2}{4}$	◆ Melodic and Harmonic 6ths

◆ Harmonizing melodies with G, D7, and C chords

The **key signature** is the sharp(s) or flat(s) located at the beginning of each staff. It indicates which notes are sharp or flat throughout the piece.

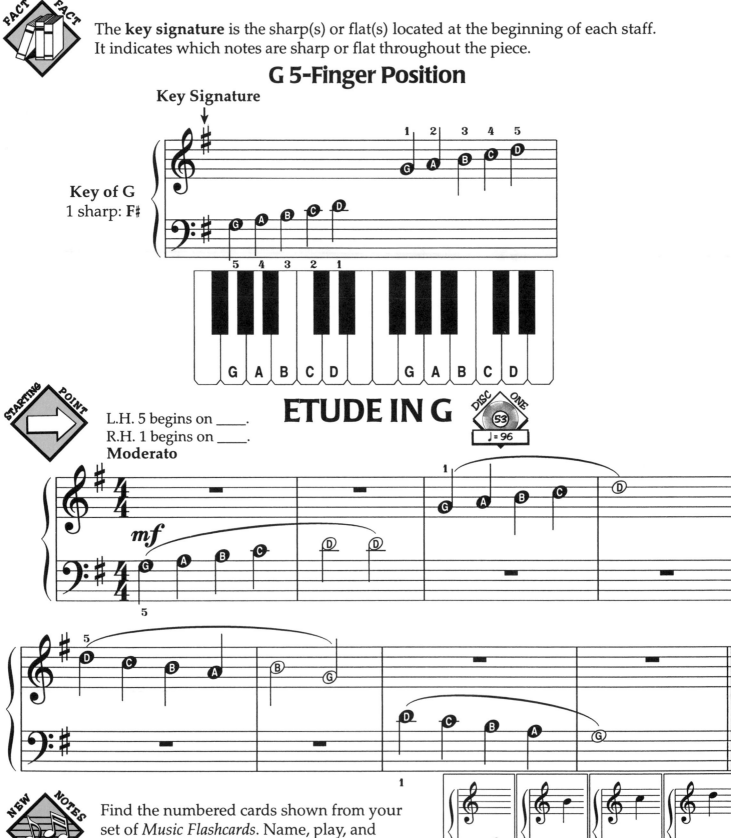

L.H. 5 begins on ____.
R.H. 1 begins on ____.

Find the numbered cards shown from your set of *Music Flashcards*. Name, play, and memorize these notes.

KP1

Time Signature

◆ The upper number indicates the number of beats (or counts) in each measure.
◆ The lower number indicates what kind of a note gets one beat (or count).

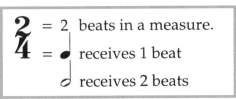

$\frac{2}{4}$	= 2 beats in a measure.
	= ♩ receives 1 beat
	= 𝅗𝅥 receives 2 beats

INTERVAL STRETCH

R.H. 1 begins on ____.
L.H. 1 begins on ____.

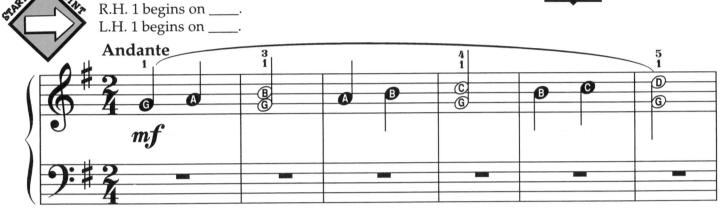

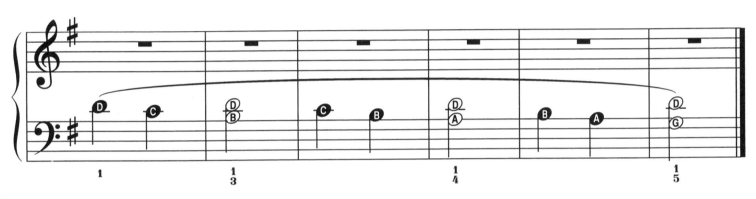

REVEILLE

L.H. 1 begins on ____.
R.H. 1 begins on ____.

Traditional Bugle Call

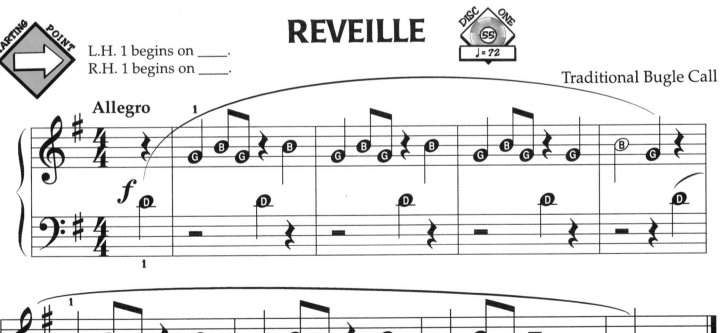

The G Chord

In the Key of G:

- ◆ The **G** Chord is built on **Degree I** which is **G**.
- ◆ There are 3 notes in the G chord: **G B D**
- ◆ **G** is the **root** of the G chord.
- ◆ **G** is called the **tonic** note or **key note**, and a chord built on G is called a **tonic chord** or a **I chord**.

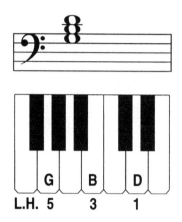

G B D
L.H. 5 3 1

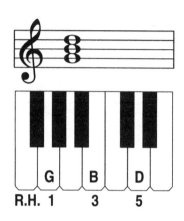

G B D
R.H. 1 3 5

The term *Aeolian Harp* comes from Aeolus, the mythological keeper of the winds. The aeolian harp was a sixteenth-century string instrument in the shape of a box, about three feet long. When set in a breezy spot, the wind allowed the strings to vibrate, producing a chord-like sound.

THE AEOLIAN HARP

Find the numbered card shown from your set of *Music Flashcards.* Name, play, and memorize this note.

Write the names of the intervals (2nd, 3rd, 4th, or 5th) in the boxes provided.

WALTZ FOR VIOLA

L.H. 1 begins on ____.
R.H. begins on a ____ chord.

LOVE SOMEBODY

R.H. 1 begins on ____.
L.H. 5 begins on ____.

Traditional
Song

Review

A. Write the interval names (2nd, 3rd, 4th, or 5th) in the boxes provided.
B. Write the letter names of the notes in the blanks.
C. Play the notes in the correct place on the keyboard.

1. **G** **B**   2.___   3.___ ___   4.___   5.___ ___

    3rd   [ ]   [ ]   [ ]   [ ]

6.___   7.___ ___   8.___   9.___ ___   10.___

    [ ]   [ ]   [ ]   [ ]   [ ]

11.___ ___   12.___   13.___ ___   14.___   15.___ ___

    [ ]   [ ]   [ ]   [ ]   [ ]

D. Draw notes up or down from the given notes to form the indicated intervals.
E. Write the letter names of the notes in the blanks.
F. Play the notes in the correct place on the keyboard.

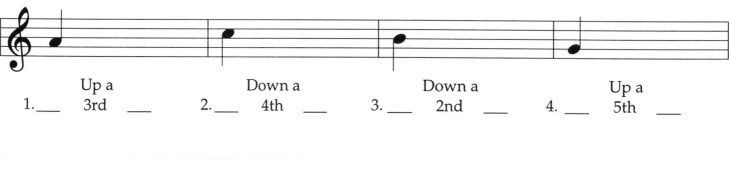

      Up a   Down a   Down a   Up a
1.___ 3rd ___   2.___ 4th ___   3.___ 2nd ___   4.___ 5th ___

      Down a   Up a   Down a   Down a
5.___ 4th ___   6.___ 3rd ___   7.___ 5th ___   8.___ 2nd ___

Legato R.H. – Staccato L.H.

Music notation often indicates that one hand is to be played legato and the other hand is to be played staccato. Mastering this technic takes concentration, coordination, and slow practice.

Practice Suggestions

1. Play hands separately first.
2. Play hands together slowly, listening for a singing legato R.H. and a soft staccato L.H.

WARM UP

R.H. 3 begins on ____.
L.H. 1 begins on ____.
L.H. 5 begins on ____.

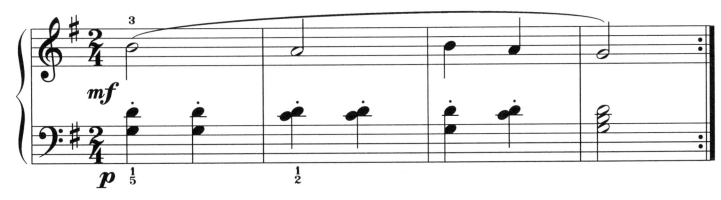

MUSETTE

R.H. 5 begins on ____.
L.H. 5 begins on ____.

Johann Sebastian Bach

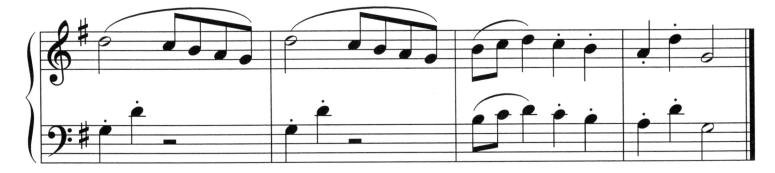

KP1

BELLS IN THE TOWER

DISC ONE 60 ♩ = 92

R.H. 5 begins on _____.
L.H. 1 begins on _____.
L.H. 5 begins on _____.

KP1

TAKE ME OUT TO THE BALL GAME

L.H. 5 begins on ____.
R.H. 4 begins on ____.

Words by Jack Norworth
Music by Albert von Tilzer

Moving to the D7 Chord

In the Key of G:

- ◆ The **D7** chord is built on **Degree V** which is **D.**
- ◆ D is called the **dominant note.**
- ◆ The **D7 chord** is also called a **dominant 7th chord** or a **V7 chord.**
- ◆ There are 4 notes in the D7 chord: **D F# A C**
- ◆ **D** is the **root** of the D7 chord.
- ◆ The number **7** means that **C** is **7** tones above **D.**

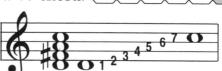

- ◆ For ease in accompanying at the introductory level, you will play a D7 chord made up of 3 notes in the arrangement shown below:

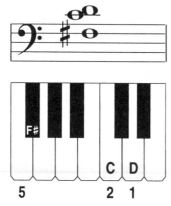

L.H. ⑤ moves **down** to **F#**

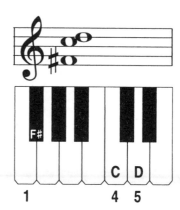

R.H. ① moves **down** to **F#**

The key signature indicates which notes are sharp or flat throughout the piece. In *Chord Etude* every F will be played as F#.

CHORD ETUDE

♩ = 96 · DISC ONE 62

L.H. 5 begins on ____.
R.H. 1 begins on ____.

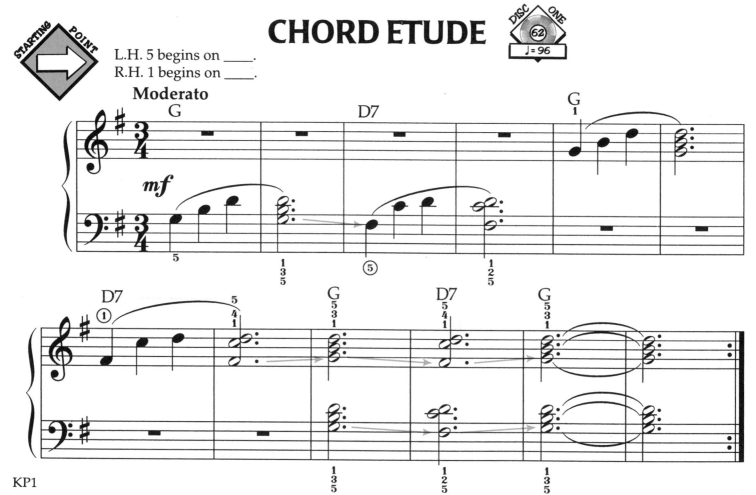

WARM UP

HUSH, LITTLE BABY

DISC ONE 63 ♩ = 96

Traditional
Lullaby

Moderato

G 3

mp Hush, lit - tle ba - by,

D7

don't say a word.

Dad - dy's gon - na buy you a

G

mock - ing bird.

If that mock - ing

D7

bird does - n't sing,

G

Dad - dy's gon - na buy you a

dia - mond ring.

p

rit.

pp

NEW NOTES Find the numbered card shown from your set of *Music Flashcards*. Name, play, and memorize this note.

KP1

Write the chord symbols (G or D7) in the boxes provided.

LIGHTLY ROW

Traditional Folk Song

Note: The second finger crosses over the first finger in both hands throughout *Stars Above*.

STARS ABOVE

R.H. 5 begins on _____.
L.H. begins on a _____ chord.

Moderato

★ *a tempo* means to return to the original tempo.

Moving to the C Chord

In the Key of G:

- ◆ The **C** chord is built on **Degree IV** which is **C**.
- ◆ C is called the **subdominant note.**
- ◆ A chord built on the subdominant note is called the **subdominant chord**, or the **IV chord.**
- ◆ C is the **root** of the C chord.
- ◆ You have already played the C chord arranged: **C E G**

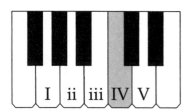
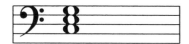

- ◆ To allow for a smooth chord progression in the Key of G, you will play the C chord in the arrangement shown below:

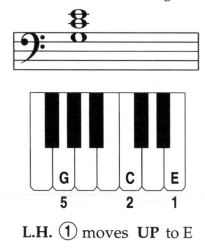

L.H. ① moves **UP** to E

R.H. ⑤ moves **UP** to E
R.H. ③ moves **UP** to C

CHORD ETUDE

Find the numbered cards shown from your set of *Music Flashcards.* Name, play, and memorize these notes.

KP1

WARM UP

AT SUNSET

Melodic and Harmonic Intervals: 6ths

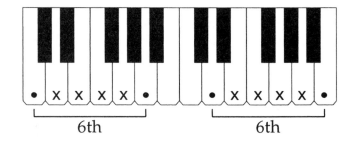

On the keyboard
A **6th skips four** white keys.

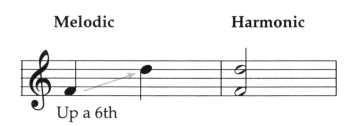

On the staff
A **6th** is written from a **line to a space**   OR   a **6th** is written from a **space to a line.**

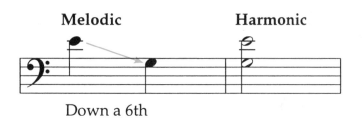

Melodic   Harmonic   Melodic   Harmonic

Down a 6th   Up a 6th

LAVENDER'S BLUE

R.H. 1 begins on ____.
L.H. begins on a ____ chord.

Allegretto

English Folk Song

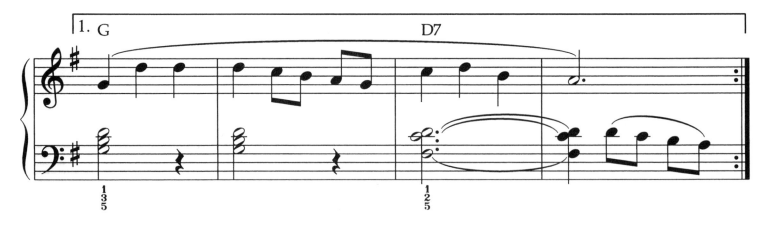

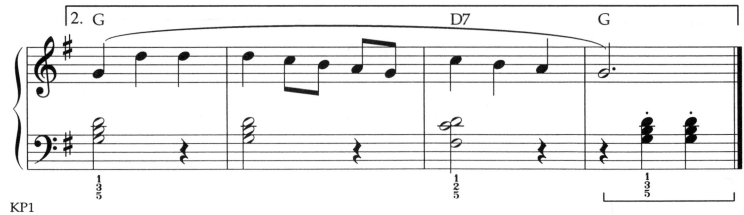

WARM UP

OH, SUSANNA

Words and Music by
Stephen Foster

Review

A. In the Key of C:
    1. The tonic note is _____.
    2. The subdominant note is ____.
    3. The dominant note is _____.

B. Write the chord symbols (C, G7, F) in the boxes provided.
C. Play the chords in the correct place on the keyboard.

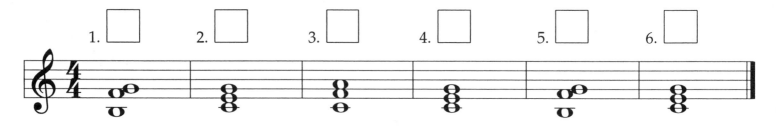

D. In the Key of G:
    1. The tonic note is _____.
    2. The subdominant note is ____.
    3. The dominant note is _____.

E. Write the chord symbols (G, D7, C) in the boxes provided.
F. Play the chords in the correct place on the keyboard.

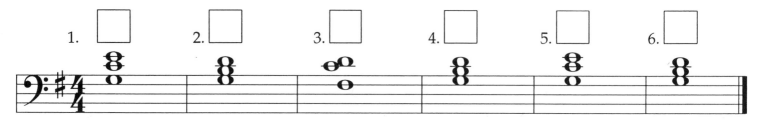

G. Write the letter names in the blanks.
H. Write the interval names (2nd, 3rd, 4th, 5th, or 6th) in the boxes provided.
I. Play the notes in the correct place on the keyboard.

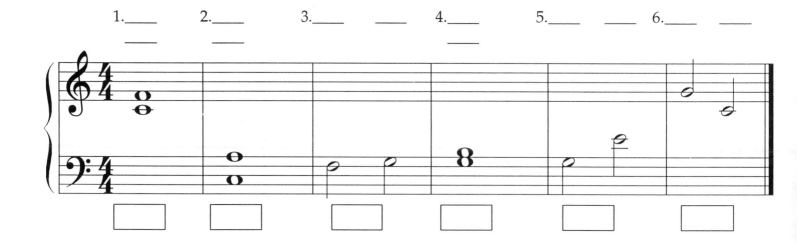

WALKING ALONG

R.H. 1 begins on ____.
L.H. begins on a ____ chord.

★ *D.C. al Fine* is an abbreviation for *Da Capo al Fine*. It means to go back to the beginning of the piece and play to the *Fine* (end).

Coda ⊕

A *Coda* is a section of a composition added as a conclusion. *D.C. al Coda* means to return to the beginning and play until the directions or the *Coda* sign ⊕ indicate to skip to the *Coda*. At that point, play the *Coda*, which ends the piece.

MORNING RAINBOW

Technic

Use a medium tempo (♩=84) when playing each of the following exercises.

HARMONIC 5THS AND 6THS

LEGATO-STACCATO INTERVALS

R.H. 1 begins on _____.
L.H. begins on a _____ chord.

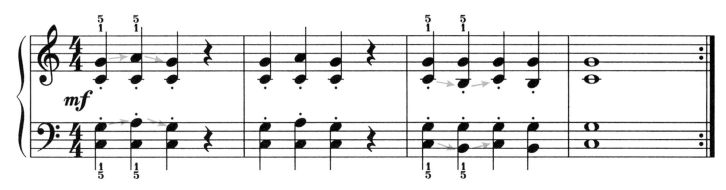

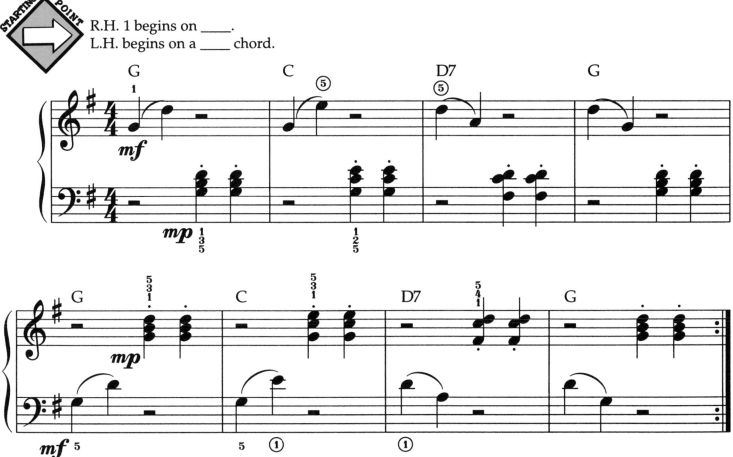

Challenge Piece

Antonio Vivaldi (1678 - 1741), Italian composer, was a priest, a violin virtuoso, a violin teacher, and a prolific composer. For most of his career, Vivaldi was the "music master" at a famous orphanage for girls called the Pio Ospedale della Pietà in Venice, where music was heavily emphasized. His duties included teaching violin lessons and composing music. Vivaldi is famous for expanding the possibilities and sounds of the violin and for his concertos. Joseph Machlis and Kristine Fornay, authors of *The Enjoyment of Music,* write: "His novel use of rapid scale passages, extended arpeggios, and contrasting registers contributed decisively to the development of violin style and technique. He played a leading part in the history of the concerto, effectively exploiting the contrast in sonority between large and small groups of players." The excerpt below is taken from the first movement, *Spring,* of *The Four Seasons. The Four Seasons* is a group of four violin concertos and is probably Vivaldi's best-known work.

R.H. 3 begins on _____.
L.H. 1 begins on _____.
L.H. 5 begins on _____.

SPRING

Antonio Vivaldi

Review

A. Write the names of the intervals (2nd, 3rd, 4th, 5th or 6th) in the boxes provided.
B. Write the letter names of the notes in the blanks.
C. Play the notes in the correct place on the keyboard.

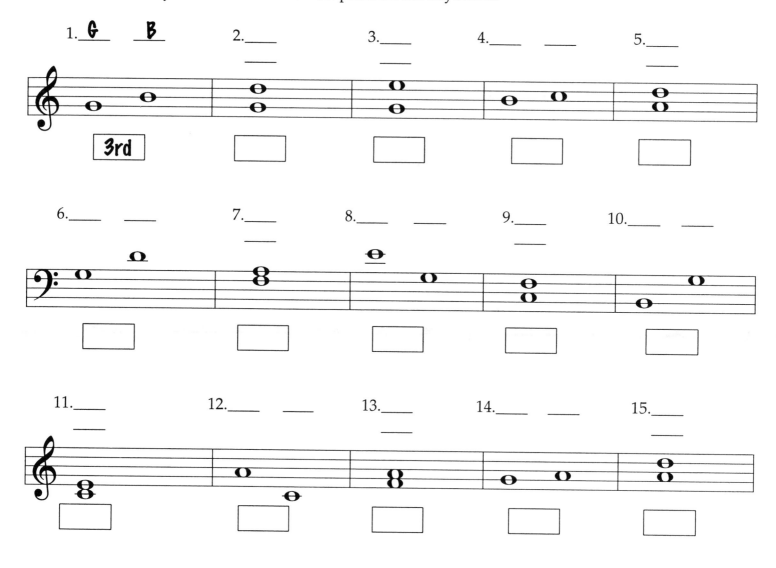

1. **G** **B**   2.___   3.___   4.___ ___   5.___

| 3rd |

6.___ ___   7.___   8.___ ___   9.___   10.___ ___

11.___   12.___ ___   13.___   14.___ ___   15.___

D. In the Key of C:
   1. The tonic note is _____.
   2. The subdominant note is _____.
   3. The dominant note is _____.

E. Write the chord symbols (C, G7, F) in the boxes provided.
F. Play the chords in the correct place on the keyboard.

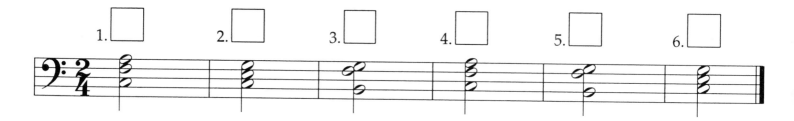

1. 2. 3. 4. 5. 6.

G. In the Key of G:
     1. The tonic note is _____.
     2. The subdominant note is _____.
     3. The dominant note is _____.

H. Write the chord symbols (G, D7, C) in the boxes provided.

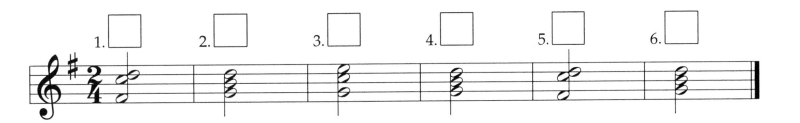

J. Draw X's on the keyboards to indicate the given notes.

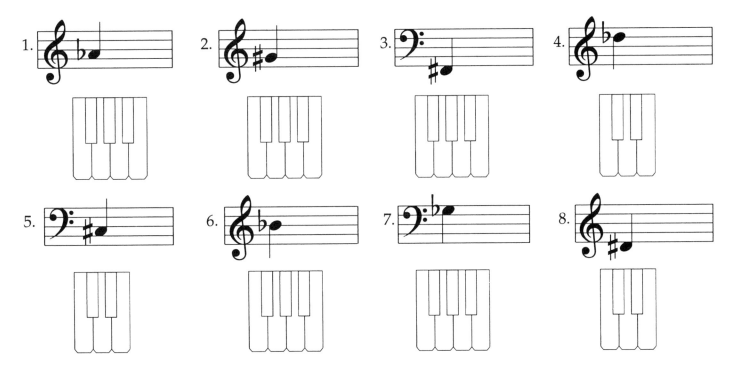

K. Harmonize.
  When playing *Evening Wind*, add L.H. chords by following the chord symbols given.

EVENING WIND

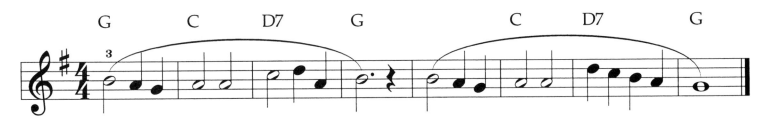

Chapter 6
New Rhythms

- ◆ Single eighth note ♪
- ◆ D. S. al Fine
- ◆ Dotted quarter note ♩.
- ◆ New Dynamics *ff* and *pp*

EIGHTH NOTE

♪ or ♪ = half of a beat

♪ ♪ = ♫ = ♩ = 1 beat

EIGHTH REST

𝄽 = one eighth rest

𝄽 = half of a beat

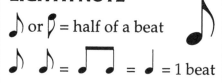

Count: 1 & 2 & 3 & 4 & 1 & 2 & 3 & 4 &

THE KING'S COURT

Steady march beat

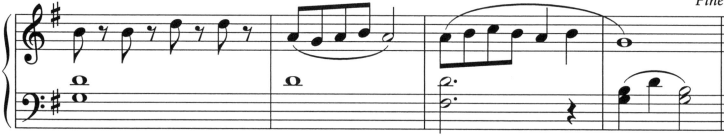

PARISIAN STREET SCENE

A dot after any note is equal to half the value of the note.

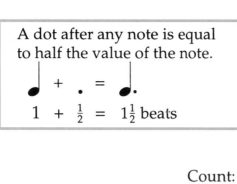

DOTTED QUARTER NOTE

Count: " **QUAR** - ter dot"
or
Count: "1 & 2"

Count: 1 & 2 & 3 & 4 &

LONDON BRIDGE

Traditional
English
Folk Song

Moderato

Lon - don Bridge is   fall - ing down,   fall - ing down,   fall - ing down,

Lon - don Bridge is   fall - ing down,   my   fair   lad - y

DECK THE HALL

Traditional
American words
to an Old Welsh Air

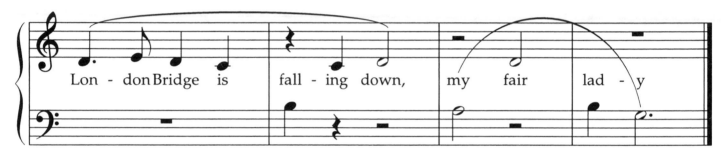

Allegretto

Deck the hall with   boughs of hol - ly,   fa la la la la   la   la la la.

AMERICA THE BEAUTIFUL

Words by Katharine Lee Bates
Music by Samuel A. Ward

Andante

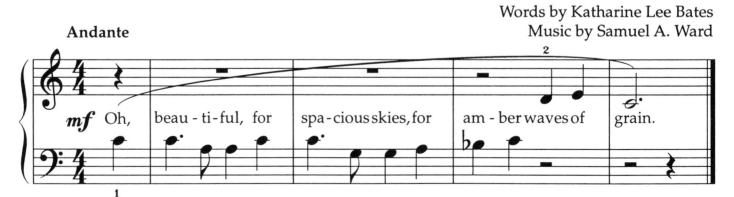

Oh,   beau - ti - ful, for   spa - cious skies, for   am - ber waves of   grain.

ANGELS WE HAVE HEARD ON HIGH

Traditional French Carol

Wolfgang Amadeus Mozart (1756 - 1791), Austrian composer, was and continues to be an unparalleled musical genius. Mozart was given harpsichord and violin lessons by his father, Leopold. By the age of five he could play and compose pieces. He learned almost by instinct and was able to reproduce melodies after one hearing. When he was six years old his father arranged for Mozart to perform throughout Europe. He displayed his remarkable musical ability to perform, sight read, improvise, and play his own compositions. Goethe, a teenager at the time, heard young Mozart perform and wrote, "I was only fourteen years old, but I see, as if I were still there, the little man with his child's sword and curly hair. . . . A phenomenon like that of Mozart remains an inexplicable thing" *(Milton Cross' Encyclopedia Of The Great Composers And Their Music).* During his brief life, he wrote numerous symphonies, operas, concertos, songs, church music, chamber music, and keyboard music. Below is an excerpt from Mozart's *Sonata in A Major, K. 331.*

SONATA THEME

Wolfgang Amadeus Mozart

D.S. al Fine

D.S. al Fine is an abbreviation for *Dal Segno al Fine.* It means to return to the *Segno* (sign 𝄋) and play until the *Fine* (end).

ALOUETTE

L.H. 5 begins on ____.
R.H. 5 begins on ____.

French-Canadian Folk Song

AMERICA

R.H. 3 begins on ____.
L.H. begins on a ____ chord.

Words by Samuel Francis Smith
to the tune *God Save the King*

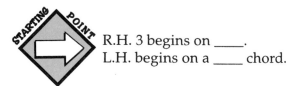

Moderato

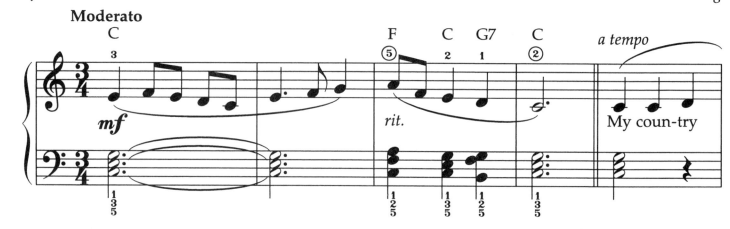

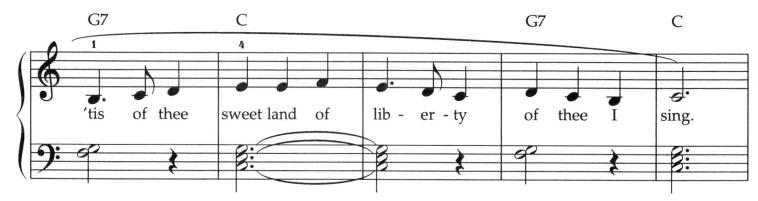

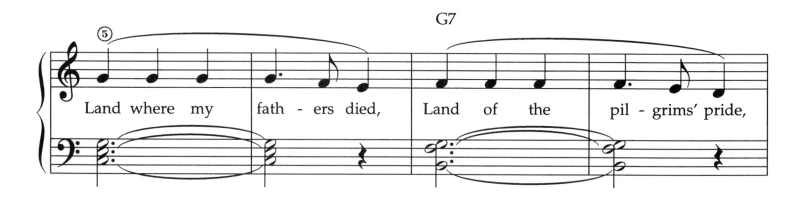

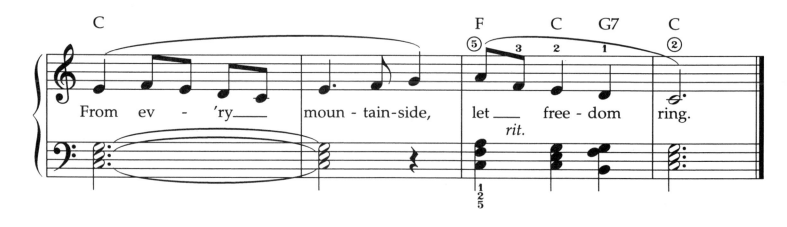

MORNING MOOD

L.H. 5 begins on ____.
R.H. 1 begins on ____.

Moderato

2nd time play both hands one octave higher.

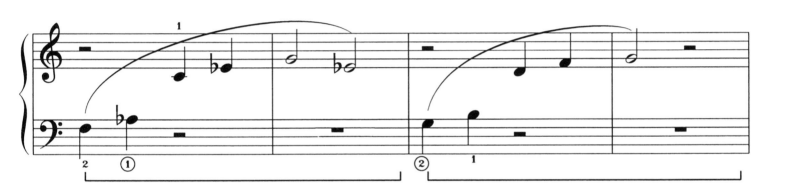

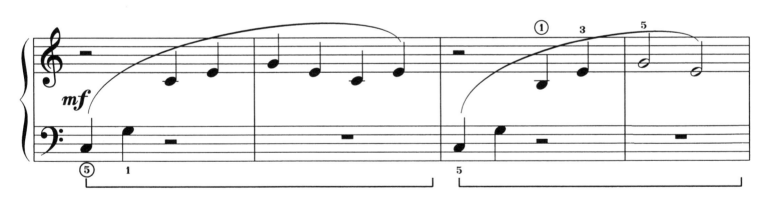

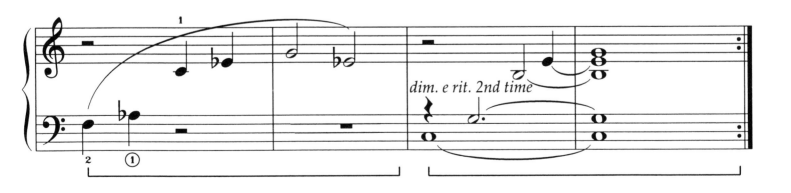

KP1

Dynamics and Shading

$\boldsymbol{ff}$ = fortissimo
very loud

$\boldsymbol{pp}$ = pianissimo
very soft

Crescendo means to start softly and gradually play louder.

Decrescendo means to start loudly and gradually play softer.

DYNAMIC CHASE

R.H. 1 begins on ____.
L.H. 1 begins on ____.
L.H. 5 begins on ____.

Mysteriously

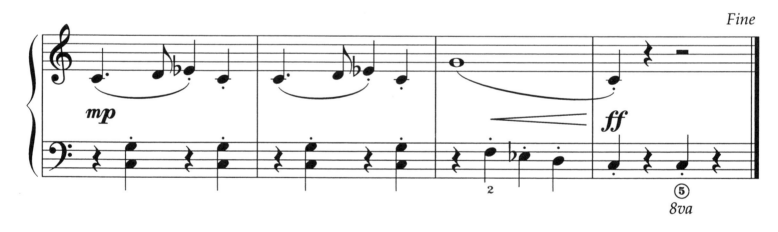

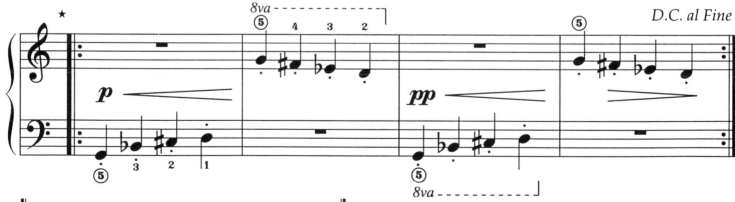

★ 𝄆 Repeat the music between the repeat signs 𝄇

KP1

Technic

1. Use a slow tempo (♩ = 50) when playing the following exercises and listen for hands playing exactly together.
2. When you are comfortable at the slow tempo, try using a medium tempo (♩ = 66).

FOUR EXERCISES

from *Opus 16*

Aloys Schmitt

Challenge Piece

THE CAISSON SONG

R.H. 5 begins on ____.
L.H. 1 begins on ____.

Words and music by
Edmund L. Gruber

Steady march beat

Find the numbered card shown from your set of *Music Flashcards*. Name, play, and memorize this note.

Review

A. Write the letter names of the notes in the blanks.
B. Play the notes in the correct place on the keyboard.

1.____   2.____   3.____   4.____   5.____   6.____   7.____

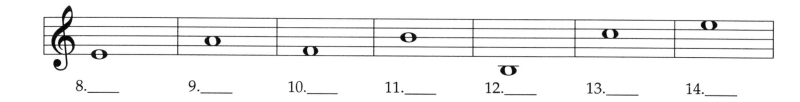

8.____   9.____   10.____   11.____   12.____   13.____   14.____

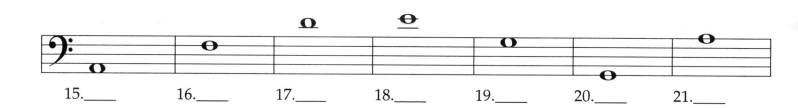

15.____   16.____   17.____   18.____   19.____   20.____   21.____

22.___ 23.___ 24.___ 25.___ 26.___ 27.___ 28.___ 29.___ 30.___ 31.___ 32.___ 33.___

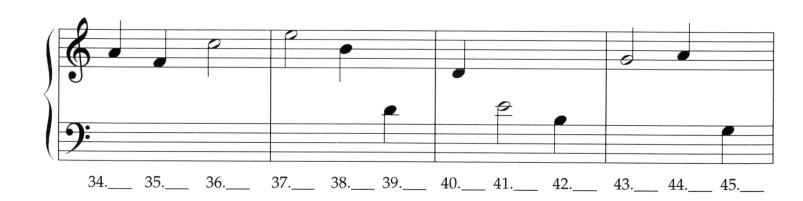

34.___ 35.___ 36.___ 37.___ 38.___ 39.___ 40.___ 41.___ 42.___ 43.___ 44.___ 45.___

C. Write the number of beats each rest or note(s) receives in $\frac{4}{4}$.

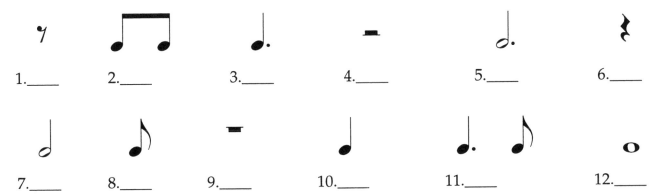

1.____ 2.____ 3.____ 4.____ 5.____ 6.____

7.____ 8.____ 9.____ 10.____ 11.____ 12.____

D. Add barlines to divide this melody into measures.
E. Play this melody on the keyboard.

F. Add one rest to complete each of the following measures.

G. Match each music example to its correct definition.

____ *D.S. al Fine*   a. slowly (walking tempo)
____ Allegro   b. moderately
____ Andante   c. repeat from the sign 𝄋 to the *Fine* (end)
____ Moderato   d. moderately fast
____ *D.C. al Fine*   e. fast
____ Allegretto   f. repeat from the beginning and play to the *Fine*
____ *a tempo*   g. return to the original tempo

H. Harmonize
   When playing *This Old Man*, add L.H. chords by following the chord symbols given.

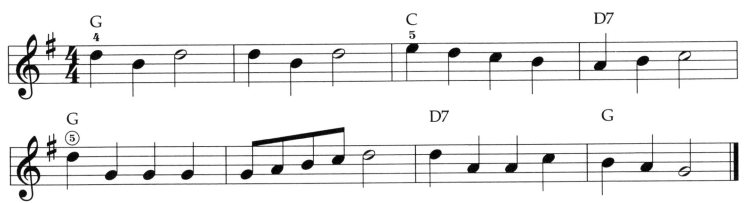

KP1

Chapter 7
Reading in F

- ◆ Reading in the Key of F
- ◆ Natural Sign ♮
- ◆ Major and minor chords
- ◆ Harmonizing melodies with F, C7, and B♭ chords.
- ◆ Group 1 keys: C G F
- ◆ 12 Bar Blues
- ◆ Overlapping pedal

The **key signature** is the sharp(s) or flat(s) located at the beginning of each staff.
The **key signature** indicates which notes are sharp or flat throughout the piece.

F 5-Finger Position

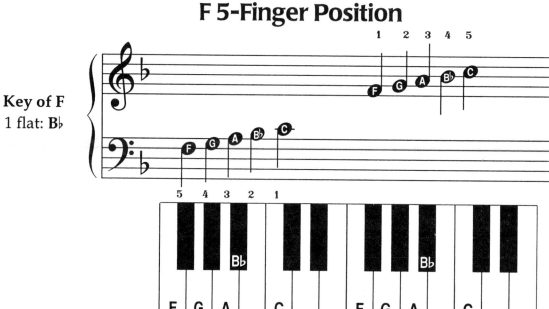

Key of F
1 flat: B♭

Note: In the key of F, play every B as B♭.

ETUDE IN F

Moderato

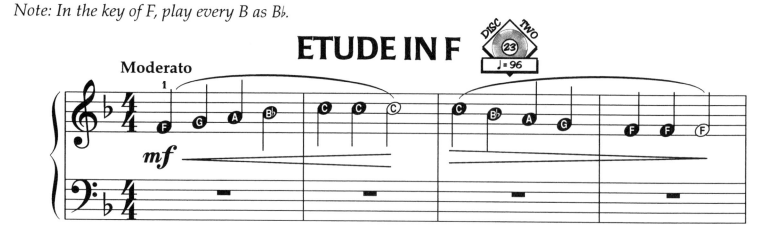

mf

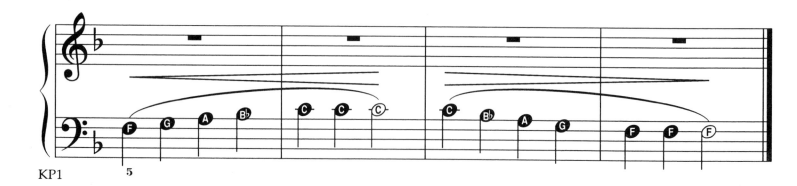

KP1

INTERVAL DANCE

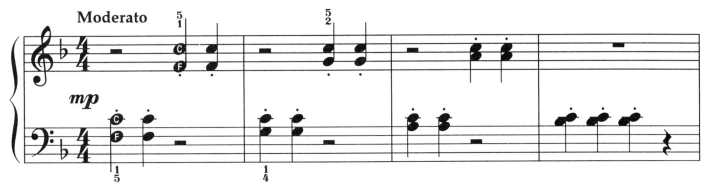

SONG OF THE SEA

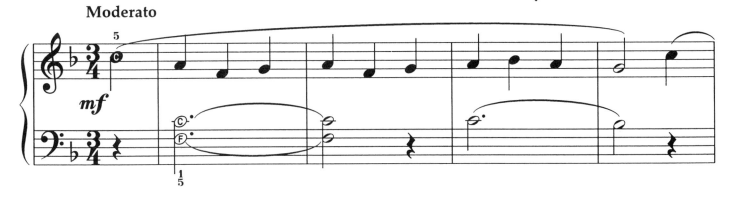

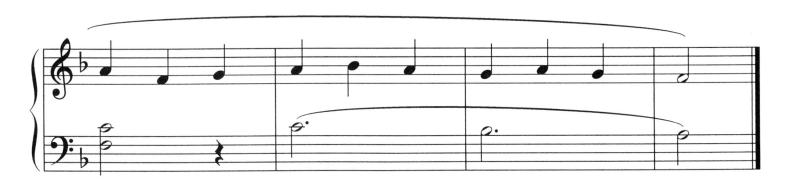

Chords in F

In the Key of F:

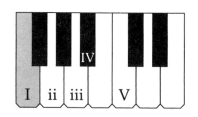

- ◆ The **F** chord is built on **Degree I** which is F.
- ◆ F is called the **tonic note**, or **key note**, and a chord built on F is called the **tonic chord** or the **I chord**.
- ◆ **F** is the **root** of the F chord.
- ◆ You have already played the F chord with the notes arranged: **C F A**
- ◆ You will now play the F chord in the arrangement shown below:

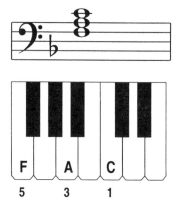
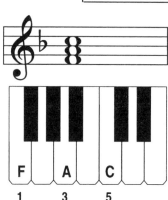

- ◆ The **B♭** chord is built on **Degree IV** which is B♭.
- ◆ B♭ is called the **subdominant note** and a chord built on B♭ is called the **subdominant chord** or the **IV chord**.
- ◆ There are 3 notes in the B♭ chord: **B♭ D F**
- ◆ **B♭** is the **root** of the B♭ chord.
- ◆ For ease in accompanying at the introductory level, you will play the B♭ chord in the arrangement shown below:

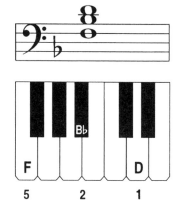
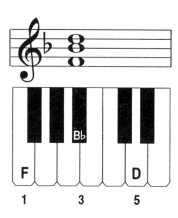

- ◆ The **C7** chord is built on **Degree V** which is C.
- ◆ The C7 chord is also called the **dominant 7th chord** or the **V7 chord**.
- ◆ There are 4 notes in the complete C7 chord: **C E G B♭**
- ◆ **C** is the **root** of the C chord.
- ◆ The number 7 means that B♭ is 7 tones above C. For ease in accompanying at the introductory level, you will play the C7 chord in the arrangement shown below:

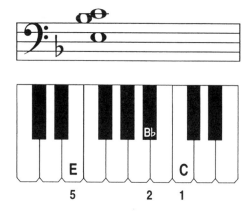
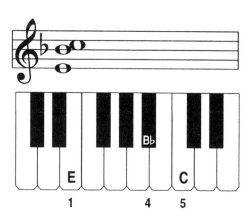

PRELUDE

L.H. 5 begins on ____.
R.H. 1 begins on ____.

Moderato

Find the numbered card shown from your set of *Music Flashcards*.
Name, play, and memorize this note.

35

KP1

WARM UP

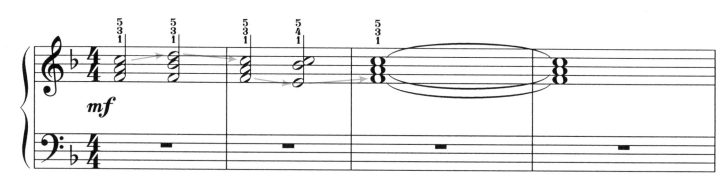

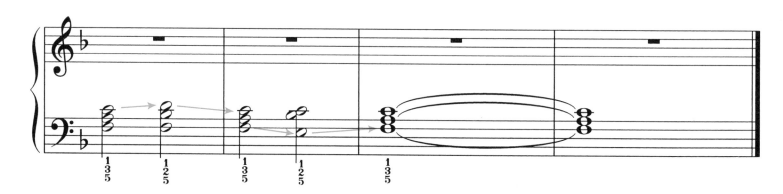

JINGLE BELLS

DISC TWO 27 ♩ = 132

STARTING POINT

R.H. 3 begins on ____.
L.H. begins on a ____ chord.

Moderato

Words and Music by
James S. Pierpont

Jin-gle bells, jin-gle bells, jin-gle all the way! Oh, what fun it

is to ride in a one-horse o-pen sleigh!___ one-horse o-pen sleigh!

Review

A. In the Key of F:

1. The tonic note is _____.
2. The root of the tonic chord (I) is _____.

3. The subdominant note is _____.
4. The root of the subdominant chord (IV) is _____.

5. The dominant note is _____.
6. The root of the dominant chord (V) is _____.

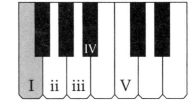

B. Write the chord symbols (F, Bb, or C7) in the boxes provided.
C. Play the chords in the correct place on the keyboard.

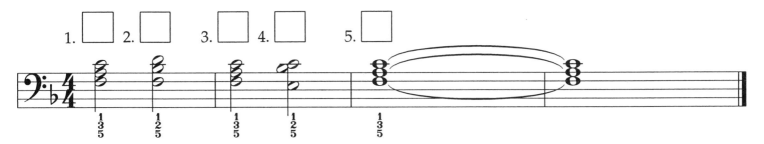

D. In the Key of G:

1. The tonic note is _____.
2. The root of the tonic chord (I) is _____.

3. The subdominant note is _____.
4. The root of the subdominant chord (IV) is _____.

5. The dominant note is _____.
6. The root of the dominant chord (V) is _____.

E. Write the chord symbols (G, C, or D7) in the boxes provided.
F. Play the chords in the correct place on the keyboard.

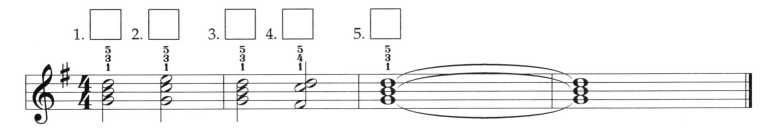

Group 1 Keys: C, G, F

You have learned to play in three keys: C, G, and F. These three keys are called the **Group 1 keys** because they all have the same look and feel in their I chords. Each chord has only **white keys**.

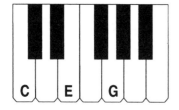 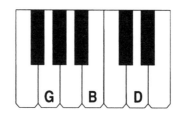 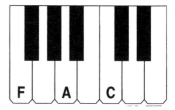

When playing the following exercise, move your hands as early as possible for each position change in order to keep a steady beat.

WARM UP

CHORD HOP

The 12 Bar Blues and Primary Chords

The **12 Bar Blues** is a form in music based on I, IV and V chords. The I, IV, and V chords are called **primary chords**. These three chords are the most important chords in any key.

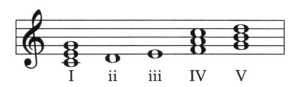

| I | ii | iii | IV | V |

Natural Sign ♮

A natural sign ♮ before a note cancels a sharp or flat. This sign indicates to play the natural (white) key.

12 Bar Blues		
I chord	=	4 measures
IV chord	=	2 measures
I chord	=	2 measures
V chord	=	1 measure
IV chord	=	1 measure
I chord	=	2 measures

THE 12 BAR BLUES

R.H. 2 begins on ____.
L.H. begins on a ____ chord.

TWILIGHT BLUES

Moderato

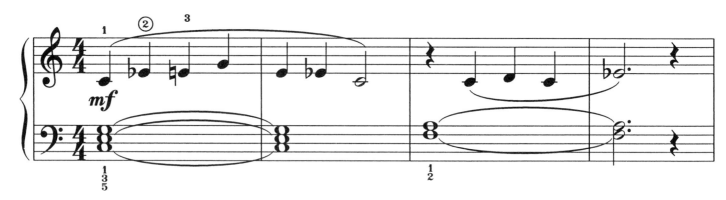

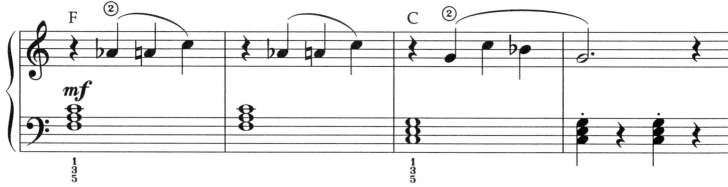

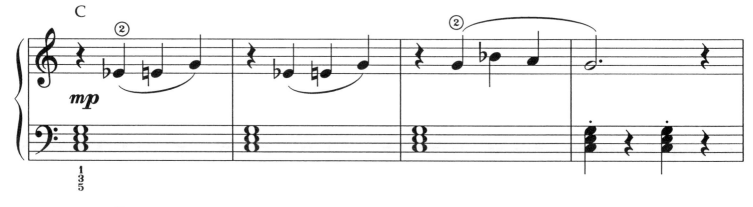

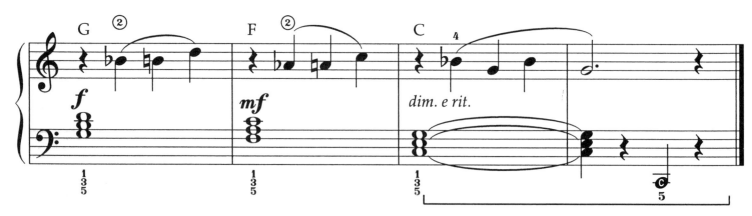

Find the numbered card shown from your set of *Music Flashcards*.
Name, play, and memorize this note.

Half Step

A **half step** is the distance from one key to the very next key, with **no key in between**.

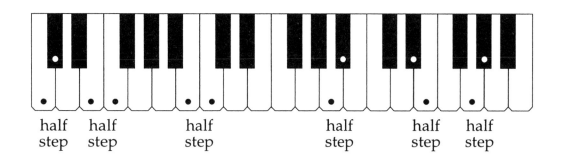

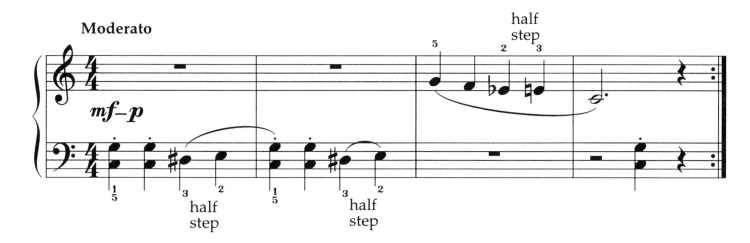

Whole Step

A **whole step** is the distance from one key to the next key, with **one key in between**.

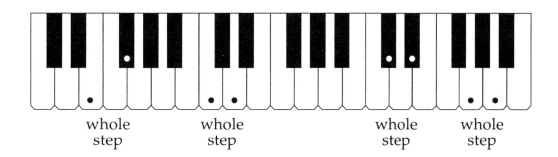

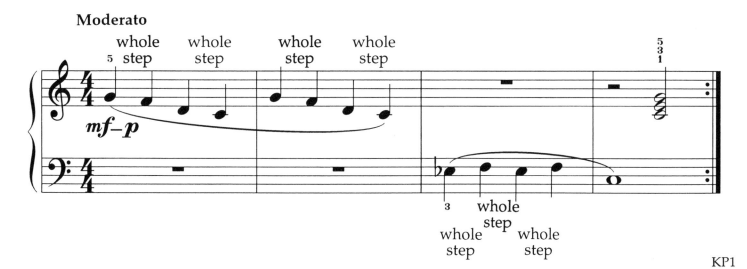

Boogie Bass Line

Notice the half steps in the following boogie bass line.

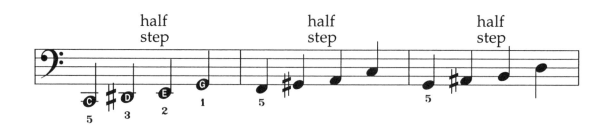

RIVERBOAT BOOGIE

L.H. 5 begins on ____.
R.H. 2 begins on ____.

Moderate boogie beat

★ For clearer reading, the circles around finger numbers will no longer be included. Be sure to check if a hand position change is needed.

cross over

Find the numbered cards shown from your set of *Music Flashcards*. Name, play, and memorize these notes.

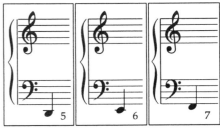

Johann Strauss, Jr. (1825 - 1899), Austrian composer, came from a musical family. His father, Johann, Sr., was the proprietor of a beer-house and dance-hall, and a conductor and composer of light music. Johann, Jr. became a musician against the will of his father, who apprenticed him to become a bookbinder. After running away from home, Johann, Jr. was finally allowed to study violin and composition. By the time he was nineteen he formed his own orchestra and performed as conductor of that group. His ensemble received instantaneous success, and Strauss composed new waltzes for their performances. He made a tour through Austria, Germany, Poland, and Russia, and in 1872 he came to America to direct concerts in Boston and New York. Strauss wrote almost five hundred dance-music pieces (waltzes, polkas, marches, gallops, etc.). He also wrote such operetta favorites as *Die Fledermaus (The Bat,* 1874) and *The Gypsy Baron* (1855), which are filled with famous melodies. Because of his numerous famous waltzes, he justly earned the title "Waltz King." The excerpt below is from Strauss' famous work *The Blue Danube Waltz.*

THE BLUE DANUBE WALTZ

L.H. 5 begins on ____.
R.H. 5 begins on ____.
R.H. 3 begins on ____.

Johann Strauss, Jr.

Waltz Tempo

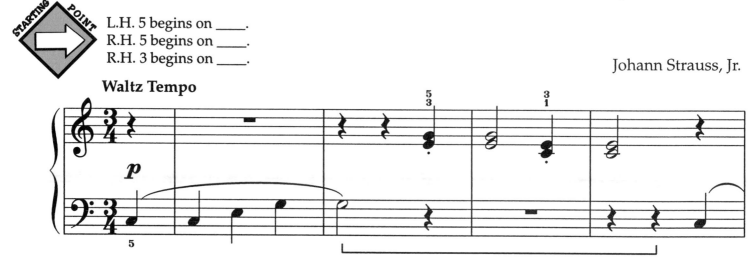

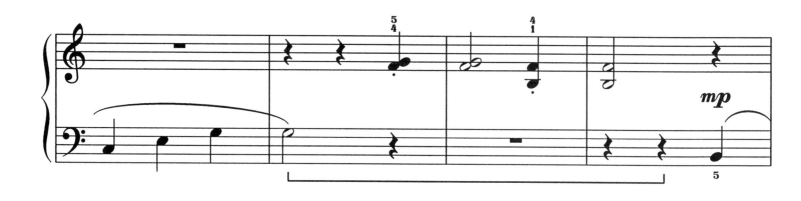

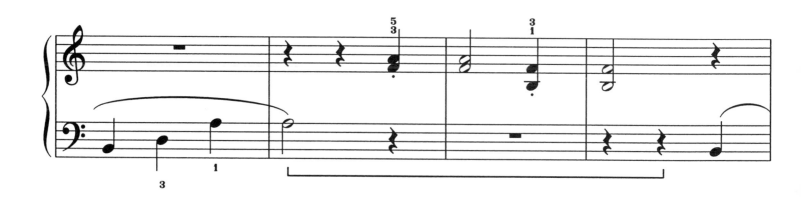

CLASSIC DANCE

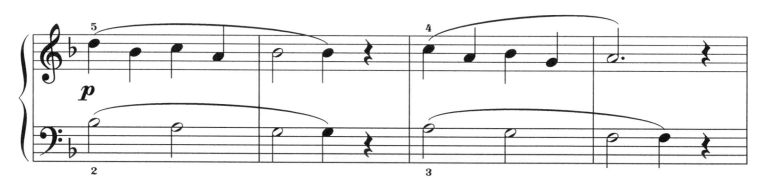

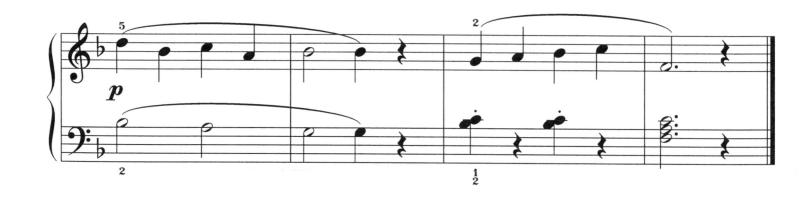

The **12 Bar Blues** follows this chord progression:

12 Bar Blues		
I chord	=	4 measures
IV chord	=	2 measures
I chord	=	2 measures
V chord	=	1 measure
IV chord	=	1 measure
I chord	=	2 measures

GOT THE BLUES

R.H. 1 begins on ____.
L.H. begins on a ____ chord.

Slow blues tempo

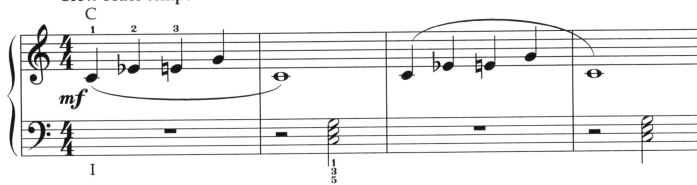

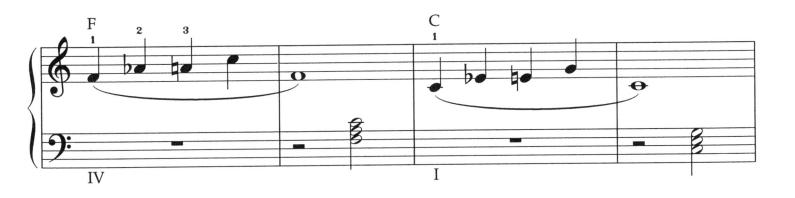

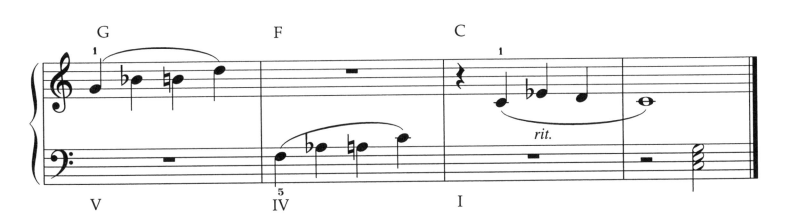

Major and Minor Chords

You have now learned three Major chords: C, G, and F.

Major chords are made up of a **Major 3rd** (4 half steps) and a **minor 3rd** (3 half steps).

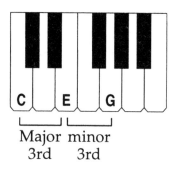 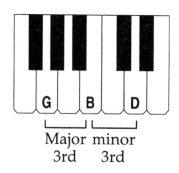 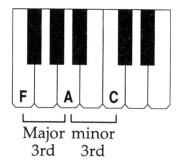

Minor chords are made up of a **minor 3rd** (3 half steps) and a **Major 3rd** (4 half steps).

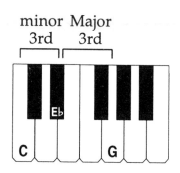 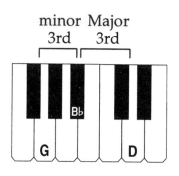 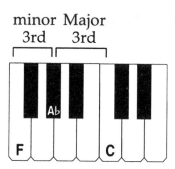

From every Major chord, a minor chord may be formed by moving the middle note of the chord down one half step.

C Major   C minor   F Major   F minor   G Major   G minor

WARM UP

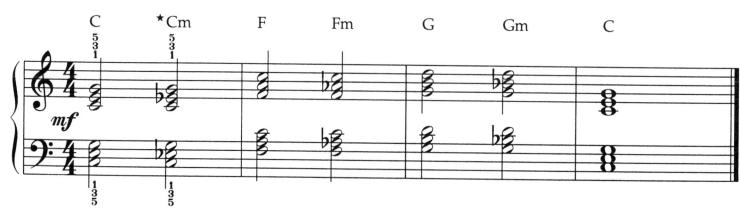

★ A lowercase "m" is used next to the letter name of the chord symbol to indicate a minor chord.

Technic

1. Use a medium tempo (♩ = 66) when playing each of the following exercises.
2. Practice hands separately first. Then practice hands together.

OCEAN WAVES

R.H. 1 begins on ____.
L.H. 5 begins on ____.

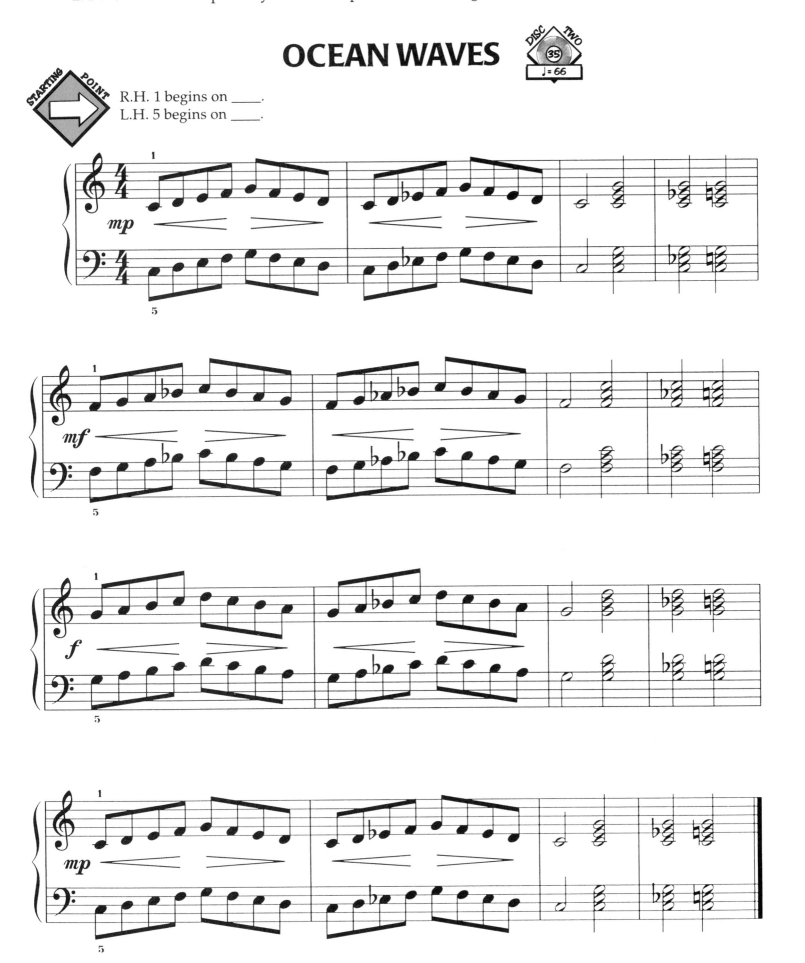

Challenge Piece

change pedal

Overlapping Pedal: The overlapping pedal is indicated by this sign:

Practice the following left hand chord progression with pedal as a warm up for *Blue Mood*.

BLUE MOOD

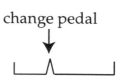

R.H. 2 begins on _____.
L.H. begins on a _____ chord.

Andante con rubato★

★ **Rubato** means that time is "borrowed," or that some tones are held longer than their actual values, while others are curtailed, in order to allow more freedom and spontaneity.

KP1

Review

A. Write the letter names of the following notes.
B. Play the notes in the correct place on the keyboard.

1. _____   2. _____   3. _____   4. _____   5. _____   6. _____
   _____   _____   _____   _____   _____   _____

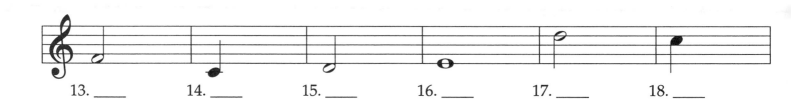

7. _____   8. _____   9. _____   10. _____   11. _____   12. _____
   _____   _____   _____   _____   _____   _____

13. _____   14. _____   15. _____   16. _____   17. _____   18. _____

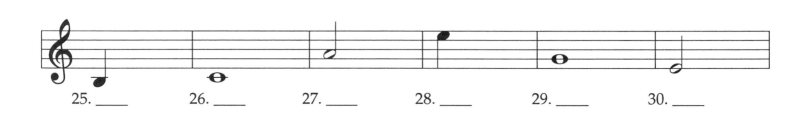

19. _____   20. _____   21. _____   22. _____   23. _____   24. _____

25. _____   26. _____   27. _____   28. _____   29. _____   30. _____

31. _____   32. _____   33. _____   34. _____   35. _____   36. _____

C. In the Key of F:

    1. The tonic note is _____.
    2. The root of the tonic chord is _____.

    3. The subdominant note is _____.
    4. The root of the subdominant chord is _____.

    5. The dominant note is _____.
    6. The root of the dominant chord is _____.

D. Write the chord symbols (F, B♭, or C7) in the boxes provided.
E. Play the chords on the keyboard.

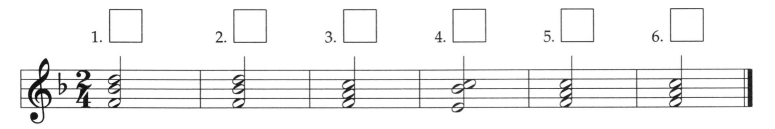

F. Identify the following as either half or whole steps.

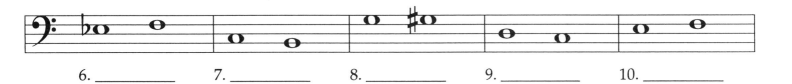

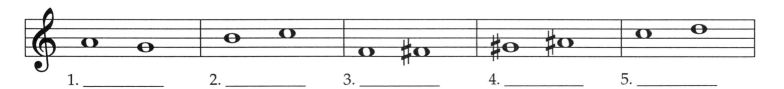

G. The Group 1 keys are _____, _____, and _____.

H. The Roman numerals for the primary chords in any key are _____, _____, and _____.

I. Harmonize
    Add your own choice of L.H. Chords (F, B♭, or C7) to the following R.H. melody line.
    Write chord symbols in the boxes provided.

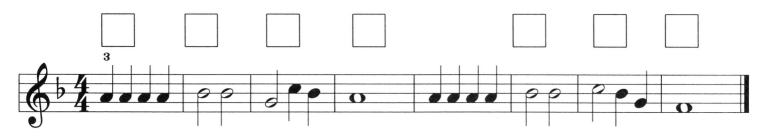

Chapter 8

Scales, Chords, and Inversions

- ◆ Melodic and Harmonic 7ths and octaves
- ◆ C Major scale
- ◆ Common Time **C**
- ◆ Chords and inversions
- ◆ A minor scale and chords
- ◆ Cut Time **₵**

Melodic and Harmonic Intervals: 7ths

On the keyboard
A **7th skips five** white keys.

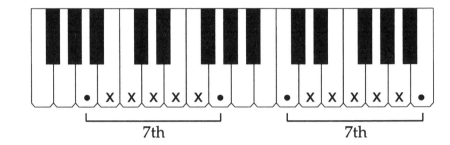

On the staff
A **7th** is written from a **line to a line**   OR   a **7th** is written from a **space to a space**.

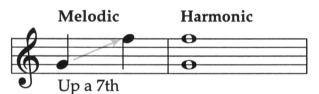
Melodic   Harmonic
Up a 7th

Melodic   Harmonic
Down a 7th

 Write the names of the intervals (5th, 6th, or 7th) in the boxes provided.

INTERVAL MARCH

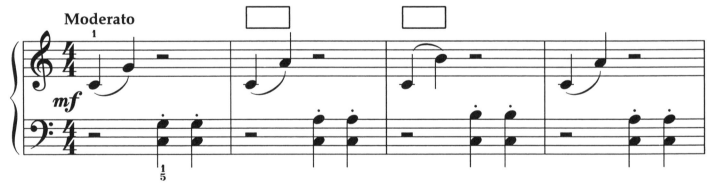

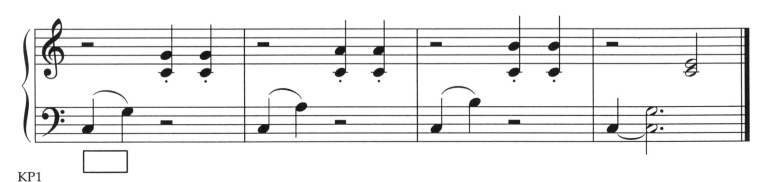

Melodic and Harmonic Intervals: Octaves

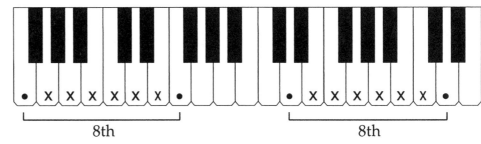

On the keyboard
An **octave skips six** white keys.

On the staff
An **octave** is written from a **line to a space**   OR   an **octave** is written from a **space to a line**.

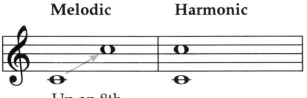

Melodic   Harmonic

Up an 8th

Melodic   Harmonic

Down an 8th

SING THE BLUES

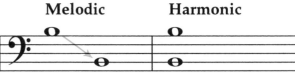

Andante

mf

mp

dim.   e   rit.

pp

KP1

Major Scale

A **Major scale** has eight tones formed in a pattern of whole and half steps. The scale is divided into two equal parts, each having four notes. Each part is called a **tetrachord**. The pattern for each tetrachord is:
whole step, whole step, half step.

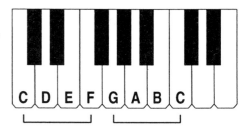

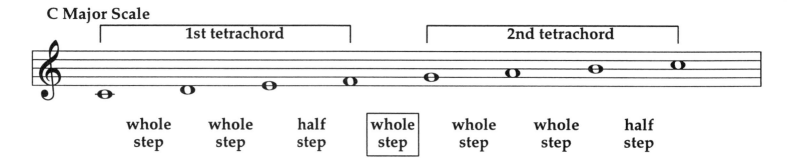

Each tetrachord is joined by a whole step.

WARM UP

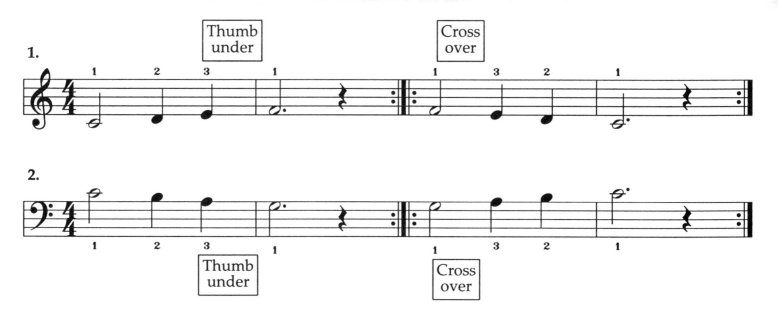

C Major Scale

Play hands separately first. **Memorize** this fingering.

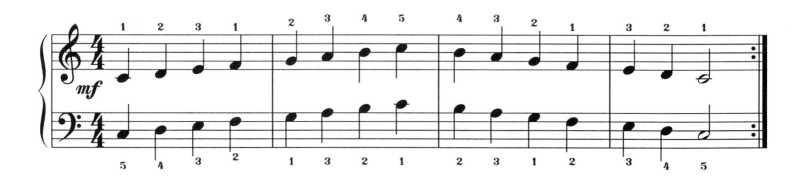

Common Time 𝄴

The symbol 𝄴, which stands for Common Time, is another way to indicate the $\frac{4}{4}$ time signature.

$$\mathbf{C} = \frac{4}{4} \begin{array}{l} = 4 \text{ beats in a measure.} \\ = \text{♩ receives 1 beat.} \end{array}$$

SCALING THE ROCKIES

DISC TWO 40 ♩ = 60

STARTING POINT

R.H. 1 begins on ____.
L.H. 1 begins on ____.

NEW NOTES

Find the numbered cards shown from your set of *Music Flashcards.*
Name, play, and memorize these notes.

38 39

KP1

Cut Time ₵

The symbol ₵, which stands for Cut Time,
is another way to indicate the ²⁄₂ time signature.

₵ = ²⁄₂ = 2 beats in a measure.
= 𝅗𝅥 receives 1 beat.

HALLELUJAH CHORUS

from the oratorio *Messiah*

George Frideric Handel

Moderato

Review

A. Write the names of the intervals in the boxes provided.

B. Play the notes in the correct place on the keyboard.

1. [ ] 2. [ ] 3. [ ] 4. [ ] 5. [ ] 6. [ ]

7. [ ] 8. [ ] 9. [ ] 10. [ ] 11. [ ] 12. [ ]

C. Identify the following notes as half steps or whole steps in the blanks provided.

D. Play the notes in the correct place on the keyboard.

1. _____ 2. _____ 3. _____ 4. _____ 5. _____ 6. _____ 7. _____ 8. _____

9. _____ 10. _____ 11. _____ 12. _____ 13. _____ 14. _____ 15. _____ 16. _____

E. Write the C Major scale ascending and descending.

F. Circle the half steps.

G. Play the scale on the keyboard.

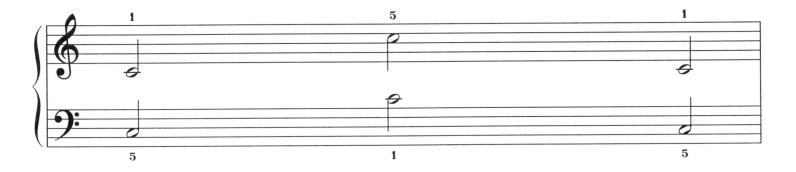

Inversions of Triads and Seventh Chords

A **triad** is a three-note chord. A **root position triad** is a triad in its most basic form. All notes are stacked in intervals of 3rds, beginning with the root located on the bottom.

An **inversion** is a different arrangement of notes in a triad. An inverted triad contains an interval of a 3rd and an interval of a 4th. The shaded note indicates the root in the inversions shown below. When the triad is inverted, the root is the **top note** of the **interval of a 4th**.

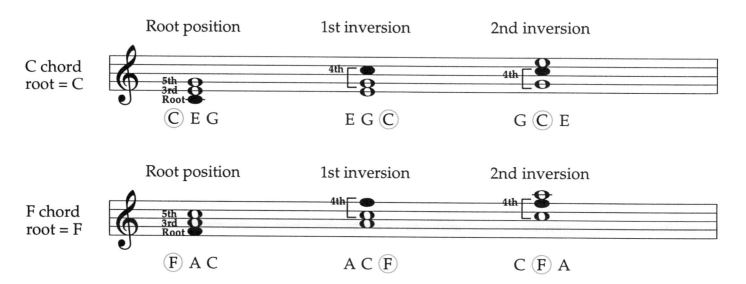

A **seventh chord** is a four-note chord. The complete G7 chord has 4 notes: **G B D F**
The G7 chord has three inversions. The shaded note indicates the root in the inversions shown below. When the chord is inverted, the root is the top note of the **interval of a 2nd**.

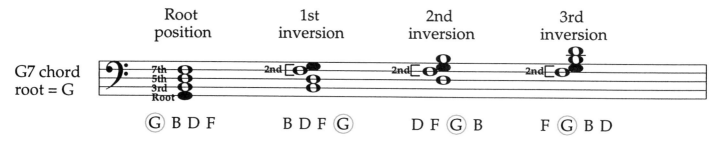

Throughout this book, you have played G7 as a three-note 1st inversion chord. For ease in accompanying at the introductory level, the D has been omitted.

WARM UP

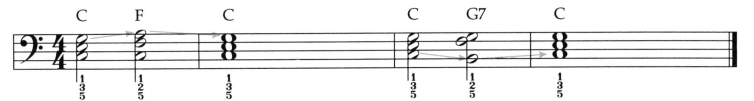

AUTUMN FEST

 L.H. begins on a _____ chord.
R.H. 3 begins on _____.

Allegro

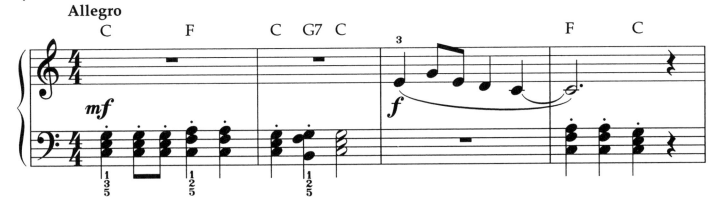

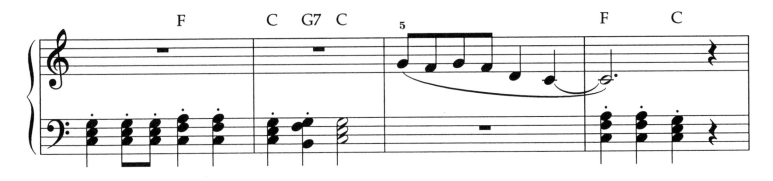

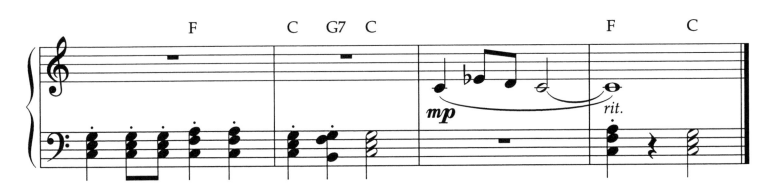

WARM UP

Joy to the World

Write chord symbols (C, F, or G7) in the boxes provided.

COUNTRY GARDENS

English Folk Dance

INTERLUDE

Relative Minor Scale

For each Major key there is a **relative minor**. The same key signature is used for both keys. The relative minor scale uses the 6th tone of the Major scale for its starting note. There are three types of minor scales. The most common form is the **harmonic minor**. The harmonic minor scale uses the same tones as the Major scale, with one exception: the 7th note in the harmonic minor scale is raised one half step.

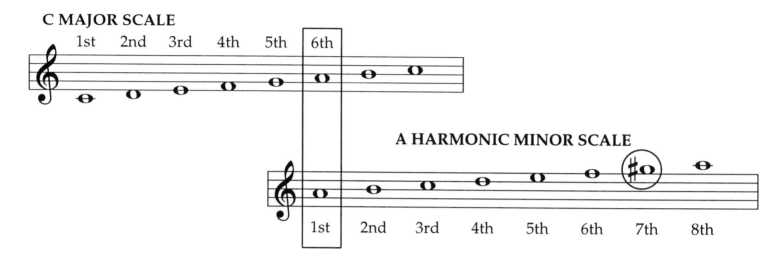

Primary Chords in the Key of A minor

Notice that chords i and iv are minor; lower case Roman numerals indicate minor.

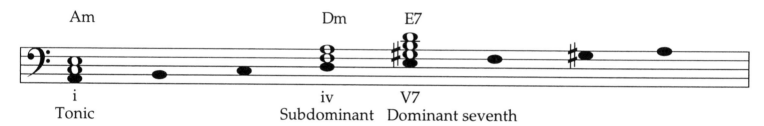

WARM UP

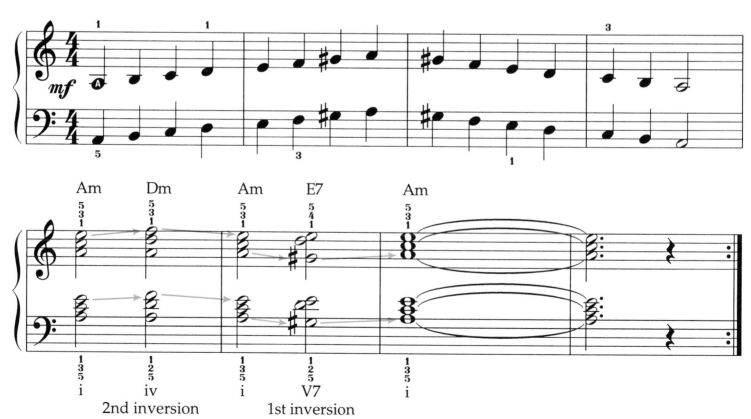

IN BAGDAD

♩ = 72

L.H. 1 begins on ____.
R.H. 1 begins on ____.

Moderato

★ *Molto* means much, or very; *dim. molto* means gradually becoming much softer.

Find the numbered card shown from your set of *Music Flashcards*.
Name, play, and memorize this note.

23

KP1

PRELUDE IN A MINOR

Moderato

★ Observe the clef changes in the left hand.

Find the numbered card shown from your set of *Music Flashcards*.
Name, play, and memorize this note.

KP1

The dotted quarter note ♩. receives 1½ beats. The eighth note ♪ receives half of a beat.

GREENSLEEVES

Traditional English

L.H. 3 begins on ____.
R.H. 1 begins on ____.

Moderato

rit.

KP1

SCARBOROUGH FAIR

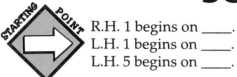

R.H. 1 begins on ____.
L.H. 1 begins on ____.
L.H. 5 begins on ____.

Traditional British Folk Song

Moderato

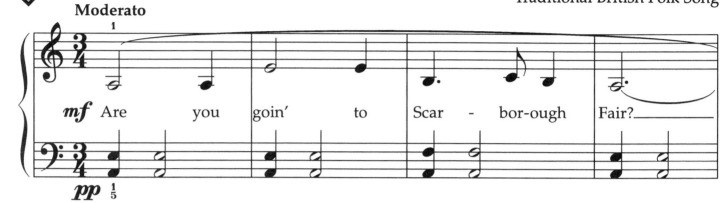

mf Are you goin' to Scar - bor-ough Fair?____

pp

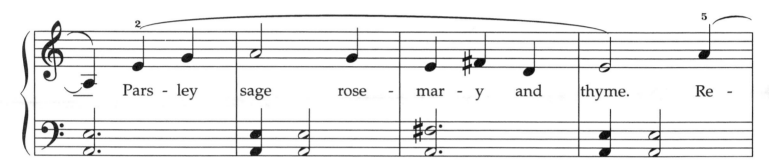

Pars - ley sage rose - mar - y and thyme. Re -

mem - ber me to one who lives there.____

She once was a true love of mine.

rit.

Find the numbered card shown from your set of *Music Flashcards.*
Name, play, and memorize this note.

KP1

22

POLOVTSIAN DANCE

from the opera *Prince Igor*

Alexander Borodin

CAROL OF THE BELLS

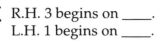

R.H. 3 begins on ____.
L.H. 1 begins on ____.

Ukrainian Carol

Allegretto

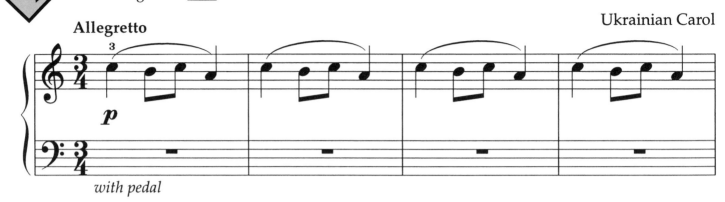

with pedal

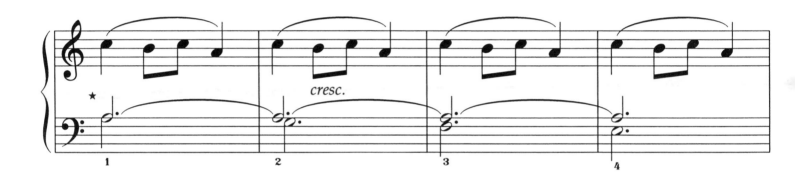

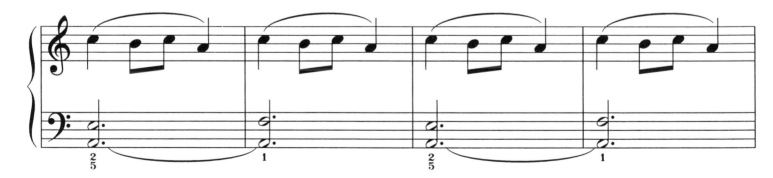

★ Hold the "A" (it is tied) for 4 measures. Notice the tie extends across the bar lines.

KP1

Scott Joplin (1868 - 1917), American composer, is thought to have been born in Texarkana, Texas in 1868. He came from a musical family. When his father bought a square grand piano, Scott taught himself how to play. By the age of eleven he had become proficient enough to attract the attention of a German music teacher who gave him lessons. At seventeen, Joplin left home to seek his fortune in music. He moved to St. Louis where he played in the "honky-tonks" on Chestnut and Market Streets from 1885 to 1893. During the latter half of the 1890's, Joplin continued to travel, perform, and develop his own style. During this period, Joplin began to write down some of the compositions he performed, and subsequently some were published. His first published composition was *Original Rags* in 1899. Joplin became the acknowledged "King of Ragtime." This style was characterized by a bouncing, steady oom-pah bass under a colorful, syncopated melody. The melody was so syncopated, in fact, that this style music of was originally called "ragged time." The excerpt below is from the rag entitled *The Entertainer*. Clamor for ragtime broke loose again in 1974 with the movie *The Sting*, which featured many of Joplin's rags arranged by Marvin Hamlisch. Practically overnight *The Entertainer* became one of the top tunes on the charts and its catchy melodies were heard everywhere.

THE ENTERTAINER

Scott Joplin

AMAZING GRACE

R.H. 1 begins on ____.
L.H. 5 begins on ____.

Words by John Newton
Traditional American Tune

★ While holding the half note "G" with R.H. 3, change to R.H. 1 without releasing the key.

Technic

Play this exercise three times a day, using three different tempos:
Slow (♩ =50), Medium (♩ =72), and Fast (♩ =96).

FINGER EXTENSION STUDY 1

from The Virtuoso Pianist

R.H. 1 begins on _____.
L.H. 5 begins on _____.

Charles-Louis Hanon

Challenge Piece

FÜR ELISE

Ludwig van Beethoven

★ *Simile* means "the same as." *Pedal simile* means to use the same pedal markings throughout the piece or until a new pedal marking is given.

Review

A. Write the names of the intervals (2nd, 3rd, 4th, 5th, 6th, 7th, or 8th) in the boxes provided.
B. Write the letter names of the notes in the blanks.
C. Play the notes in the correct place on the keyboard.

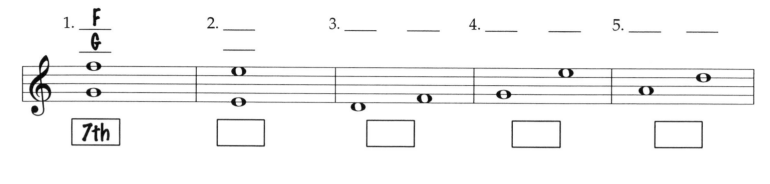

1. **F** / **G**   2. ___   3. ___ ___   4. ___ ___   5. ___ ___

7th   [ ]   [ ]   [ ]   [ ]

6. ___   7. ___   8. ___ ___   9. ___ ___   10. ___

[ ]   [ ]   [ ]   [ ]   [ ]

D. Identify the following as either half or whole steps.

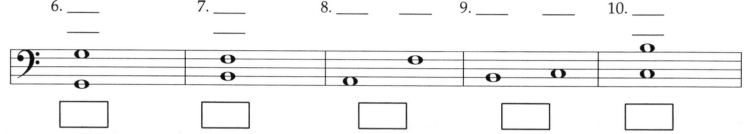

1. _____   2. _____   3. _____   4. _____   5. _____   6. _____

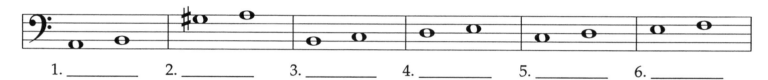

7. _____   8. _____   9. _____   10. _____   11. _____   12. _____

E. Write the C Major Scale ascending and descending. Circle the half steps.

F. Write the A harmonic minor scale ascending and descending. Circle the half steps.

G. Write the letter names of the notes in the blanks.

H. Play the notes in the correct place on the keyboard.

1. ____   2. ____   3. ____   4. ____   5. ____   6. ____   7. ____

8. ____   9. ____   10. ____   11. ____   12. ____   13. ____   14. ____

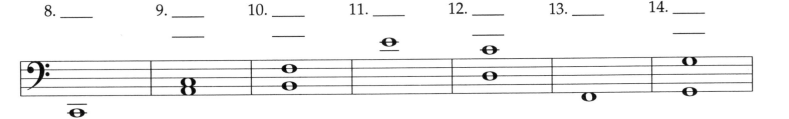

15. ____   16. ____   17. ____   18. ____   19. ____   20. ____   21. ____

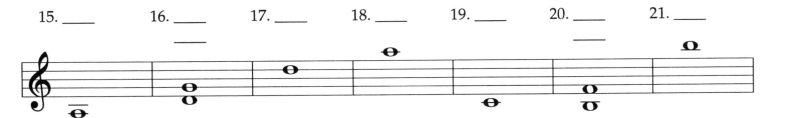

22. ____   23. ____   24. ____   25. ____   26. ____   27. ____   28. ____

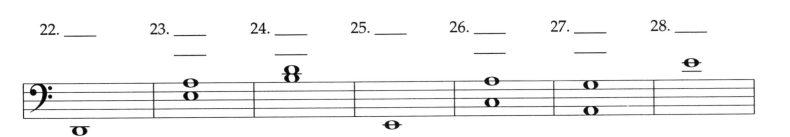

29. ____   30. ____   31. ____   32. ____   33. ____   34. ____   35. ____

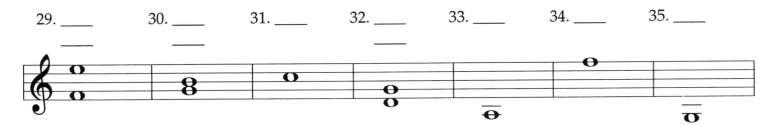

I. Harmonize

Add your own choice of L.H. chords (C, F, or G7) to the following R.H. melody line.
Write chord symbols in the boxes provided.

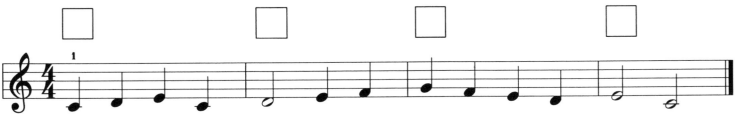

Music Dictionary

Term	Sign or Abbreviation	Meaning
Allegretto *(p. 49)*		moderately fast
Allegro *(p. 49)*		fast
Andante *(p. 49)*		slowly (walking tempo)
A tempo *(p. 75)*		return to the original tempo
Block Chord *(p. 14)*		notes in a chord played simultaneously
Broken Chord *(p. 14)*		notes in a chord played one at a time
Chord Progression *(p. 35)*		two or more chords played consecutively
Chord Symbol *(p. 35)*		a letter name placed over a note to indicate a chord that could be played with that note
Clef *(p. 16)*		
Treble Clef	𝄞	the staff sign used for middle and high tones
Bass Clef	𝄢	the staff sign used for middle and low tones
Coda *(p. 82)*	⊕	a section at the end of a composition added as a conclusion
Common Time *(p. 127)*	c	another way to indicate the $\frac{4}{4}$ time signature
Cut Time *(p. 128)*	¢	another way to indicate the $\frac{2}{2}$ time signature
Crescendo *(p. 96)*	*cresc.* <	gradually play louder
Da Capo al Coda *(p. 82)*	*D.C. al Coda* ⊕	return to the beginning and play until the coda sign ⊕ indicates to skip to the coda ⊕
Da Capo al Fine *(p. 81)*	*D.C. al Fine*	return to the beginning and play to the *Fine*
Dal Segno al Fine *(p. 93)*	*D.S. al Fine*	return to the sign (𝄋) and play to the *Fine*
Damper Pedal *(p. 29)*		the pedal on the right that is used to sustain tones
Decrescendo *(p. 96)*	*decresc.* >	gradually play softer
Degrees *(p. 32)*		the Roman numerals that name the tones within each key
Diminuendo *(p. 45)*	*dim.*	gradually play softer
Dominant Seventh Chord *(p. 37, 72, 104, 134)*		a seventh chord built on Degree V of the scale
Dominant Note *(p. 34)*		Degree V within any key
Dynamics *(p. 22)*		signs in music that indicate how loudly or softly to play
Fermata *(p. 43)*	⌢	A sign indicating a pause in music. Hold the note or notes under the fermata sign longer than their original time value
Fine *(p. 81)*		the end
Flat Sign *(p. 45)*	♭	a sign indicating to play the nearest key to the left
Forte *(p. 22)*	*f*	loud
Fortissimo *(p. 96)*	*ff*	very loud
Grand Staff *(p. 16)*		an arrangement of two staffs connected by a brace, the upper staff usually with a treble clef and the lower staff usually with a bass clef
Half Step *(p. 111)*		the distance from one key to the very next key with no key in between
Harmonic Minor Scale *(p. 134)*		A scale which uses the same tones as the relative Major scale with one exception: the 7th tone in the harmonic minor scale is raised one half step
Interval *(p. 21)*		the distance between two notes
Inversion *(p. 130)*		a different arrangement of notes in a chord
Key Signature *(p. 64)*		the sharps or flats located at the beginning of each staff
Legato *(p. 27)*		smooth and connected tones, usually indicated by a slur
Major Chord *(p. 118)*		a chord made up of a Major 3rd (4 half steps) and a minor 3rd (3 half steps)
Major Scale *(p. 126)*		eight tones formed in a pattern of whole and half steps: whole, whole, half, whole, whole, whole, half
Mezzo Piano *(p. 22)*	*mp*	medium soft
Mezzo Forte *(p. 22)*	*mf*	medium loud
Minor Chord *(p. 118)*		a chord made up of a minor 3rd (3 half steps) and a Major 3rd (4 half steps)

Natural Sign *(p. 109)* . . . . ♮ . . . . a sign before a note which cancels a sharp or flat

Note Values . . . . indicate the duration of each tone

    Eighth Note *(p. 88)* . . . . ♪

    Two Eighth Notes *(p. 54)* . . . . ♫

    Quarter Note *(p. 8)* . . . . ♩

    Dotted Quarter Note *(p. 90)* . . . . . ♩.

    Half Note *(p. 8)* . . . . ♩

    Dotted Half Note *(p. 14)* . . . . ♩.

    Whole Note *(p. 12)* . . . . o

Octave Sign *(p. 57)* . . . . *8va* . . . . a sign indicating to play one octave higher or one octave lower

Pedal Sign *(p. 29)* . . . . └──────┘ . . . . a sign indicating when to press and lift the damper pedal

Phrase *(p. 27)* . . . . a musical thought indicated by a slur

Piano *(p. 22)* . . . . *p* . . . . soft

Pianissimo *(p. 96)* . . . . *pp* . . . . very soft

Relative Minor Scale *(p. 134)* . . . . eight tones formed in a pattern of whole and half steps using the 6th tone of the Major scale for its starting note

Repeat Sign *(p. 14)* . . . . ॥ . . . . a sign indicating to repeat (play again) from the beginning of a piece

Repeat Signs *(p. 96)* . . . . ॥: :॥ . . . . signs indicating to repeat the music between the pairs of dots and barlines

Rest Signs *(p. 18)* . . . . indicate measured silence in music

    Eighth Rest *(p. 88)* ૭

    Half Rest *(p. 18)* . . . . ▬

    Quarter Rest *(p. 18)* ૨

    Whole Rest *(p. 18)* . . . . ▬

Rhythm *(p. 8)* . . . . combination of short and long tones

Ritardando *(p. 45)* . . . . *rit.* . . . . gradually slow down

Root *(p. 32)* . . . . the note from which a chord originates

Root Position *(p. 130)* : . . . . a chord in its most basic form: root on the bottom, other notes stacked in intervals of thirds

Rubato *(p. 120)* . . . . time is "borrowed," or some tones are held longer than their actual values, while others are curtailed, in order to allow more freedom and spontaneity

Sharp Sign *(p. 51)* . . . . ♯ . . . . a sign before a note indicating to play the nearest key to the right

Simile *(p. 147)* . . . . the same as

Slur *(p. 27)* . . . . a curved line over or under two or more different notes that are to be played legato (smooth, connected)

Staccato *(p. 58)* . . . . ♩ ♩ . . . . a dot placed over or under a note indicating to play in a short or detached manner

Staff *(p. 16)* . . . . a group of five horizontal lines on which notes are placed

Subdominant Chord *(p. 40)* . . . . a chord built on Degree IV in any key

Subdominant Note *(p. 40)* . . . . Degree IV in any key

Tempo *(p. 49)* . . . . rate of speed

Tetrachord *(p. 126)* . . . . four tones formed in a pattern of whole and half steps: whole, whole, half

Tie *(p. 23)* . . . . a curved line that connects notes on the same line or space. Play the first note only and hold it for the value of both notes

Time Signature *(p. 17)* . . . . the two numbers written at the beginning of each piece

Tone *(p. 4)* . . . . sound of a definite pitch

Tonic Chord *(p. 32)* . . . . a chord built on Degree I in any key

Tonic Note or Key Note *(p. 32)* . . . . Degree I in any key

Triad *(p. 130)* . . . . three-note chord

Upbeat *(p. 39)* . . . . a note (or notes) that come before the first full measure

Whole Step *(p. 111)* . . . . the distance from one key to the next key, with one key in between

Answer Key for Review Pages

Chapter 1

Page 9
A.

1. F	9. C
2. D	10. B
3. B	11. E
4. G	12. F
5. E	13. G
6. A	14. D
7. C	15. A
8. D	16. C

Page 10
A.

1. D
2. B
3. G
4. C
5. A
6. E
7. F

B.

1. quarter note
2. half note

Page 15
A.

1. D	9. D
2. G	10. G
3. B	
4. E	
5. A	
6. C	
7. F	
8. A	

B.

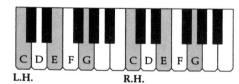

L.H.   R.H.

C.

1. ♩   2. ♩   3. ♩.   4. o

Page 19

1. G	9. C	17. C
2. E	10. G	18. G
3. C	11. D	19. D
4. F	12. C	20. G
5. D	13. F	21. E
6. G	14. E	22. C
7. F	15. G	23. G
8. E	16. D	24. F

Chapter 2

Page 20
A.

1. D
2. E
3. G
4. C
5. F

B.

1. F
2. D
3. E
4. C
5. G

C.

1. 2
2. 1
3. 4
4. 1
5. 3
6. 2
7. 4

D.

E.

F.

Page 22
2nd, 2nd, 3rd, 2nd

Page 24
A. and B.

1. F, E, down a 2nd	9. E, D, down a 2nd
2. C, E, up a 3rd	10. G, E, down a 3rd
3. E, G, up a 3rd	
4. D, C, down a 2nd	
5. F, G, up a 2nd	
6. F, G, up a 2nd	
7. E, C, down a 3rd	
8. D, F, up a 3rd	

D. and E.

1. 2nd, F, G	4. 3rd, C, E
2. 3rd, E, G	5. 3rd, E, G
3. 3rd, C, E	6. 2nd, F, G

Page 24 continued

G. and H.

1. C 3rd E   2. G Down a 2nd F   3. D Up a 3rd F   4. F Down a 2nd E

5. C Up a 2nd D   6. F Down a 3rd D   7. E Up a 3rd G   8. G Down a 2nd F

Page 28

A. and B.

1. C, F, up a 4th
2. G, C, down a 5th
3. D, G, up a 4th
4. C, G, up a 5th
5. F, C, down a 4th
6. C, F, up a 4th
7. G, C, down a 5th
8. G, D, down a 4th

9. C, G, up a 5th
10. D, G, up a 4th

D. and E.

1. 4th, C, F
2. 5th, C, G
3. 4th, D, G
4. 4th, C, F
5. 5th, C, G
6. 4th, D, G

G. and H.

1. C Up a 5th G   2. D Up a 3rd F   3. F Down a 2nd E   4. G Down a 4th D

5. F Down a 3rd D   6. G Down a 5th C   7. C Up a 4th F   8. E Up a 2nd F

Page 30

A.

1. D	9. D	17. G
2. F	10. F	18. E
3. E	11. C	
4. C	12. E	
5. G	13. C	
6. D	14. E	
7. G	15. F	
8. E	16. D	

C. and D.

1. F, E, down a 2nd
2. C, F, up a 4th
3. D, F, up a 3rd
4. G, C, down a 5th
5. F, G, up a 2nd
6. F, D, down a 3rd
7. E, F, up a 2nd
8. C, G, up a 5th

9. G, D, down a 4th
10. E, G, up a 3rd
11. F, G, up a 2nd
12. C, G, up a 5th
13. E, C, down a 3rd
14. F, C, down a 4th
15. G, D, down a 4th

Page 31

F.

1. 4
2. 4
3. 1
4. 2
5. 3
6. 1
7. 2

G.

H.

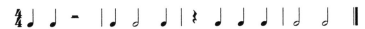

I.

J.

1. tie
2. slur
3. slur
4. tie

K.

1. forte = loud
2. mezzo forte = medium loud
3. mezzo piano = medium soft
4. piano = soft

154

Chapter 3

Page 38

A.
1. C
2. G

B.
1. G7
2. C
3. G7
4. C

Page 43
F, C, F, C

Page 46

A.

C.
1. D♭   9. D♭
2. D♭   10. F♭
3. F♭   11. E♭
4. E♭   12. E♭
5. E♭   13. D♭
6. D♭   14. D♭
7. D♭
8. D♭

Page 47

E. and F.
1. 3rd, B, D   8. 4th, C, F
2. 4th, F, C   9. 5th, C, G
3. 3rd, E, G   10. 2nd, E, D
4. 3rd, D, F
5. 5th, C, G
6. 3rd, A, F
7. 2nd, F, G

H.
1. F   9. G7
2. C   10. C
3. G7
4. G7
5. C
6. C
7. F
8. C

Page 50

A. and B.
1. A, G, down a 2nd   9. G, D, down a 4th
2. B, C, up a 2nd   10. G, C, down a 5th
3. F, B, up a 4th   11. F, C, up a 5th
4. G, A, up a 2nd   12. A, B, up a 2nd
5. B, G, down a 3rd   13. A, F, down a 3rd
6. F, D, down a 3rd   14. B, F, down a 4th
7. E, G, up a 3rd   15. G, B, up a 3rd
8. C, F, up a 4th

D. and E.

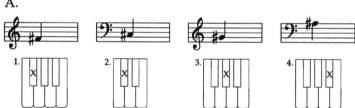

Page 53

A.

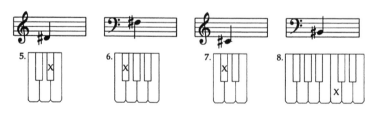

C.
1. F♯   9. C♯
2. C♯   10. D♯
3. D♯   11. C♯
4. C♯   12. A♯
5. A♯   13. G♯
6. G♯   14. F♯
7. F♯
8. F♯

Page 56

A.
1. 1
2. 2
3. 2
4. 1
5. 4
6. 1
7. 3
8. 4

B.

C.

D.

E.
1. C
2. G7
3. C
4. F
5. C
6. F
7. C
8. G7
9. C

Page 62

A. and B.

1. 3rd, A, C	9. 2nd, F, G
2. 4th, G, C	10. 5th, C, G
3. 2nd, C, D	11. 2nd, G, A
4. 4th, F, B	12. 4th, F, B
5. 5th, C, F	13. 3rd, C, A
6. 3rd, D, F	14. 5th, D, A
7. 3rd, G, E	15. 3rd, B, G
8. 4th, C, F	

D.

1. G7	9. C
2. C	10. G7
3. F	11. C
4. C	
5. F	
6. C	
7. G7	
8. F	

Page 63

F.

1.

2.

3.

G.

H.
C
A
B
D

Chapter 5

Page 67

2nd, 3rd, 2nd, 4th, 2nd, 3rd

Page 68

A. and B.

1. 3rd, G, B	9. 5th, A, E
2. 4th, A, D	10. 2nd, B, C
3. 2nd, C, B	11. 3rd, D, B
4. 5th, G, D	12. 4th, A, D
5. 3rd, B, D	13. 4th, C, G
6. 4th, G, C	14. 2nd, B, C
7. 2nd, B, A	15. 5th, B, E
8. 3rd, B, D	

D. and E.

Page 74

G, D7, G, G, D7, D7, G, G, D7, G

Page 80

A.

1. C
2. F
3. G

B.

1. G7
2. C
3. F
4. C
5. G7
6. C

D.

1. G
2. C
3. D

E.

1. C
2. G
3. D7
4. G
5. C
6. G

G. and H.

1. 4th, C, F
2. 6th, C, A
3. 2nd, F, G
4. 3rd, G, B
5. 6th, G, E
6. 5th, G, C

Page 86

A. and B.

1. 3rd, G, B	9. 4th, C, F
2. 5th, G, D	10. 6th, B, G
3. 6th, G, E	11. 3rd, C, E
4. 2nd, B, C	12. 6th, A, C
5. 4th, A, D	13. 3rd, F, A
6. 5th, G, D	14. 2nd, G, A
7. 3rd, F, A	15. 4th, A, D
8. 6th, E, G	

D.

1. C
2. F
3. G

E.

1. F
2. C
3. G7
4. F
5. G7
6. C

Page 87

G.

1. G
2. C
3. D

H.

1. D7
2. G
3. C
4. G
5. D7
6. G

J.

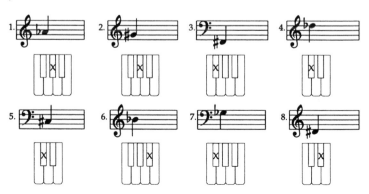

Chapter 6

Page 100
A.

1. B	10. F	19. G	28. B	37. E
2. A	11. B	20. G	29. G	38. B
3. E	12. B	21. A	30. F	39. D
4. C	13. C	22. C	31. D	40. D
5. D	14. E	23. A	32. B	41. E
6. G	15. A	24. B	33. A	42. B
7. B	16. F	25. D	34. A	43. G
8. E	17. D	26. E	35. F	44. A
9. A	18. E	27. D	36. C	45. G

Page 101
C.

1. $\frac{1}{2}$	9. 4
2. 1	10. 1
3. $1\frac{1}{2}$	11. 2
4. 2	12. 4
5. 3	
6. 1	
7. 2	
8. $\frac{1}{2}$	

D.

F.

G.

C
E
A
B
F
D
G

Chapter 7

Page 107
A.

1. F
2. F
3. B♭
4. B♭
5. C
6. C

B.

1. F
2. B♭
3. F
4. C7
5. F

D.

1. G
2. G
3. C
4. C
5. D
6. D

E.

1. G
2. C
3. G
4. D7
5. G

Page 122
A.

1. F, C	10. C, F	19. D	28. E
2. G, B	11. E, C	20. E	29. G
3. F, G	12. B, D	21. F	30. E
4. E, B	13. F	22. A	31. G
5. A, D	14. C	23. D	32. E
6. G, E	15. D	24. E	33. F
7. B, C	16. E	25. B	34. G
8. A, F	17. D	26. C	35. D
9. G, B	18. C	27. A	36. C

Page 123
C.

1. F
2. F
3. B♭
4. B♭
5. C
6. C

Page 123 continued

D.
1. B♭
2. B♭
3. F
4. C7
5. F
6. F

F.
1. Whole	9. Whole
2. Half	10. Half
3. Half	
4. Whole	
5. Whole	
6. Whole	
7. Half	
8. Half	

G.
C, G, F

H.
I, IV, V

Chapter 8

Page 124
6th, 7th, 5th

Page 129
A.
1. 6th	7. 5th
2. 5th	8. 7th
3. 7th	9. 7th
4. 8th	10. 5th
5. 6th	11. 2nd
6. 8th	12. 6th

C.
1. Whole	9. Whole
2. Half	10. Whole
3. Half	11. Half
4. Whole	12. Whole
5. Half	13. Half
6. Whole	14. Whole
7. Half	15. Whole
8. Whole	16. Whole

E. and F.

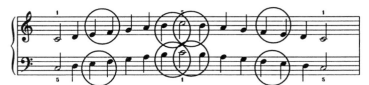

Page 132
C
F
G7
C
F
C
C
F
G7
C

Page 148
A. and B.
1. 7th, G, F	8. 6th, A, F
2. 8th, E, E	9. 2nd, B, C
3. 3rd, D, F	10. 7th, C, B
4. 6th, G, E	
5. 4th, A, D	
6. 8th, G, G	
7. 5th, B, F	

Page 148 continued

D.

1. Whole	7. Whole
2. Half	8. Half
3. Half	9. Whole
4. Whole	10. Whole
5. Whole	11. Whole
6. Half	12. Half

E. and F.

Page 149

1. A	10. B, F	19. C	28. E
2. F	11. E	20. B, F	29. F, E
3. E, E	12. D, C	21. B	30. G, B
4. B, F	13. F	22. D	31. C
5. C	14. G, G	23. E, A	32. D, G
6. C, G	15. A	24. B, D	33. A
7. E	16. D, G	25. E	34. F
8. C	17. D	26. C, A	35. G
9. A, C	18. A	27. A, G	